W9-CHR-730

Getting Started with the IBM PC and XT

David Arnold
and the Editors of PC World

PC World Library
Published by
Computer Book Division
Simon & Schuster, Inc.
New York

Copyright © 1984 by David Arnold
and PC World Communications, Inc.

All rights reserved, including the right of
reproduction in whole or in part in any form.

Published by the Computer Book Division
of Simon & Schuster, Inc.
Simon & Schuster Building
Rockefeller Center
1230 Avenue of the Americas
New York, New York 10020

Simon & Schuster and colophon are registered
trademarks of Simon & Schuster, Inc.
PC World and colophon are trademarks of
PC World Communications, Inc.

Portions of Chapters 9 and 10 were
contributed by Seth Novogrodsky.

Manufactured in the United States of America

10 9 8 7 6 5 4 3 2 1

Library of Congress Cataloging in Publication Data
Arnold, David [date]
    Getting started with the IBM PC and XT.
    Includes index.
    1. IBM Personal Computer. 2. IBM Personal Computer
XT. I. PC World Communications, Inc. II. Title.
III. Title: Getting Started with the I.B.M. P.C. and X.T.
QA76.8.I2594A76 1984   001.64   84-1377
ISBN 0-671-49277-2

Contents

Foreword

The Editors of PC World are proud to inaugurate the PC World Library with *Getting Started with the IBM PC and XT.* As publishers of the most authoritative and informative magazine about the IBM PC, XT, and compatible computers, PC World has introduced computing to millions of people; in partnership with Simon & Schuster, we now have the opportunity to reach millions more readers through PC World Books.

In planning, writing, and designing both books and magazines, the staff of PC World seeks to present information that is timely, useful, and easy to understand. Our emphasis is on excellence of information and quality of presentation, and we believe that this book and the others that follow in our series will offer readers the best possible perspective and instruction for using computers in their work and their leisure.

The PC World Library features practical books relating to the IBM PC and XT, including *How to Buy an IBM PC, XT, or PC-Compatible Computer; Hardware for the IBM PC and XT; Desktop Applications for the IBM PC and XT; Communications for the IBM PC and XT;* and *The Fully Powered PC.* Three additional books will feature the IBM PCjr: *Getting Started with the IBM PCjr; Learning and Having Fun with the IBM PC and PCjr;* and *Logo for the IBM PC and PCjr.* One other book, *Hands On,* will offer a collection of practical tips and articles from *PC World* magazine.

We welcome you to these pages and invite your participation by letting us know how this book or others have been useful or not so useful, and what topics you would like to see covered in future books from PC World and Simon & Schuster.

David Bunnell
Publisher, PC World

Preface

The goal of *Getting Started with the IBM PC and XT* is to help you put the computer to work easily and effectively. In planning this book with the Editors of PC World and in writing it, I have chosen examples and exercises designed to make you not only computer literate, but also computer competent and computer comfortable.

This book is intended to complement the manuals that are supplied with the IBM PC and XT, not to replace them. The manuals are valuable reference sources, and they cover more materials than our book has attempted. But manuals are meant to be reference tools, rather than teaching tools, and this book is intended to teach, to demonstrate, and to orient you to the whole sphere of computing.

Acknowledgments

Whoever said that writing is a lonely profession didn't write about computers. To acknowledge everyone who contributed to this effort would itself nearly require a book. But I want to single out a few people who deserve special thanks: Jeremy Joan Hewes and her colleagues at PC World Books, Seth Novogrodsky and Lindy Wankoff; Michael Baldigo, Susan Garfin, Wanda Pitts, and Nancy Small of Sonoma State University; Ray Young of the San Francisco PC Users Group; John Holmes of the Marin/Sonoma PC Users Group; Barbara Elman of *WP News;* Robert Gelber of OCLI; Gary Steffes of Micro Techniques; and two people who introduced me to computers two decades ago—Kay Pool, of the University of Iowa Computer Center and QUESTO, and Paul M. Krasno, of General Electric.

While it is traditional for authors to thank their families for supporting them through the process of turning a book from an idea into a set of floppy disks, I trust that Betty, Jerome, and Jeffrey will understand how much more than just traditional are my appreciation and love for them.

A Note to Readers
Each book in the PC World Library offers instructions and examples for using the IBM PC, XT, and certain compatible computers and other components. Although the Editors of PC World have consistently tried to provide explanations for every possible configuration of a PC or XT system, we have established certain criteria for a "standard" PC system discussed throughout this book. Unless otherwise noted, we assume that the PC has two floppy disk drives and that the disk operating system is PC-DOS 2.00.

Whenever special instructions or examples are needed for systems that differ from this standard, the Editors have included them or referred readers to an additional source of information. For example, special sections of the book are devoted to systems that use a hard disk, including the XT and IBM Expansion Unit, and to advanced features of PC-DOS that are especially useful with hard disks.

Getting Started with the IBM PC and XT

The World of Personal Computing

In 1983, as you may recall, *Time* magazine, instead of picking a "Man of the Year," chose the computer as "Machine of the Year." *Time's* article noted five motivations for spending money: necessities, investments, self-improvement, memories, and impressing friends, and added that owning a computer satisfies all five categories.

But which computer? The same week that *Time* made its announcement *InfoWorld,* the influential microcomputer newsweekly, announced its award for product of the year. The winner was the IBM Personal Computer. "Other products were also in the running," an *InfoWorld* editor wrote, "but none could compete with the IBM for votes."

Several months later, in a cover story on IBM entitled "The Colossus That Works," *Time* summed up the reason for IBM's success by quoting James Marston, American Airlines' vice president for data processing: "You can take any specific piece of hardware or software and perhaps do better than IBM, but across the board IBM offers an unbeatable system."

That one word, *system,* is the key to the PC's strength. If you are under the impression that an IBM Personal Computer consists of three pieces of *hardware*—a keyboard, a system unit, and a monitor—you're only partly right. Those are the most obvious parts of the PC. To be more than a collection of boxes, a computer needs at least one other element, preferably two.

The second element of a computer system is the *software,* the instructions or "programs" that tell it what to do. Whatever computer someone buys, he or she will end up with these two components.

Only a few brands of computers have the third useful element: a *community.* Community in this sense doesn't mean a geographical area such as Boca Raton, Florida, where IBM developed and now builds the PC. It means the organizations and services that have arisen among people who use the PC. That support is as valuable to the PC owner as the other two components.

The existence of this community is one of the things that makes the PC a landmark in the history of microcomputers and personal computing. The first landmark was a hardware development, the introduction of the first widely known microcomputer, the Altair, in January 1975. As the Altair and other early microcomputers began to catch on, hobbyists developed games, languages, and other programs for them. But microcomputers weren't of much practical use until another landmark, a software development, took place in 1979: the introduction of *VisiCalc.* The success of the Apple II computer was as much a result of the availability of *VisiCalc* as it was a tribute to the computer itself. Suddenly, business people and professionals could do tasks faster and better, and do things that were previously impossible, by investing a few thousand dollars in hardware, a few hundred dollars in software, and a few dozen hours in deciphering the documentation.

But what author Christopher Evans in 1979 called "the micro millennium" was at best peeking around the corner. It didn't break into the open until IBM, America's eighth largest corporation, rocked the world in August 1981 by announcing the IBM PC. The skeptics kept silent. America, and soon the world, had to take the micro seriously.

For a few months the PC lacked software. Observers agreed that the machine was an excellent piece of hardware, but because it pioneered the use of the 8088 microprocessor chip, at first only a few programs were able to run on it (one was *VisiCalc*).

Very quickly, however, the PC showed its true power. Although it has the power to have a memory capacity several times greater than its predecessors and the power to store millions of items of information, search files, and "crunch numbers" with extreme speed, the ultimate measure of the PC's power is the range of tasks it can perform. With a rush that amazed the computer's champions and critics alike, programmers seemed to drop whatever else they were doing to create new programs or modify existing ones for the PC.

The same thing happened in the hardware arena. Within months of the PC's release, scores of manufacturers had introduced hardware enhancements such as plug-in circuit boards that gave the PC more memory, functions, and flexibility than IBM had provided. Other manufacturers were turning out an endless array of covers, furniture, keyboard accessories, pedestals, and glare shields for the PC, in quantities and varieties unimaginable just months before.

But all that—hardware for the inside, software for the inside, and more hardware for the outside—was only part of the community that developed. Almost instantly, several computer magazines added monthly columns covering the PC, and within months three magazines hit the stands that were devoted solely to the needs of the new PC user. These publications have since been followed by other magazines as well as by scores of books on the PC. Where the Altair owner had to solve his or her problems alone or with the help of a handful of equally faithful and isolated devotees, the IBM owner had help on all sides. Not the least of this help came from PC user groups. Scores of clubs sprang up around the country, devoted to sharing information, programs, and often buying power.

Thus, the IBM PC is really a three-dimensional computer system consisting of hardware, software, and community. *Getting Started with the IBM PC and XT* introduces you to these dimensions. Chapter 1 familiarizes you with the hardware. The next several chapters cover software, including the PC's operating system (PC-DOS), choosing and using applications programs, and a brief introduction to programming. Most PC users buy their machines to run professionally developed and commercially available software, so this book will not try to turn you into a programmer. Yet a brief introduction to the subject will improve your understanding of ready-made programs and the PC as a whole.

Later chapters return to hardware, with detailed discussions of hard disks and other components. Finally, after you have gotten to know the PC's hardware and software, Chapter 13 introduces you to the community that has developed around the PC. Because no single book can do justice to the full range of the PC's capabilities, this concluding chapter also suggests where to go next.

A Guided Tour
of the PC and XT

When I go to a new city for the first time, I like to start my visit with a half-day bus tour. Even though such tours always seem to spend too much time at places that don't interest me and not enough time at those that do, I find guided tours a convenient and efficient way to get oriented. Later I can return to the places I want to know better, without worrying if I am going to miss something essential.

This chapter is just such a guided tour. Its purpose is to orient, not necessarily to satisfy. Most of the topics are covered in depth in later chapters and in the manuals that accompany the PC. Some of the topics are also covered in other volumes in the PC World Library. This tour will give you the familiarity you need to start putting your PC through its paces.

"Gaul as a whole," a Roman tour guide might tell you, "is divided into three parts." So is the IBM PC: the system unit, the monitor, and the keyboard. These parts are the essential hardware of the computer. Less central hardware items, such as printers, modems, and joysticks, are called *peripherals* (see Figure 1.1).

The System Unit

The *system unit* is the heart of the computer. It contains the central processing unit (CPU), the part that manipulates numbers, words, and other information. It also contains memory components, which

Figure 1.1 *An IBM PC with peripheral devices, including a printer, a modem, and a joystick.*

store data, and *ports,* the inlets and outlets through which data pass on the way to and from the outside world (input and output). One of the input ports is connected to the keyboard, and one of the output ports is connected to the monitor. In this sense, the computer's operation is very much like a bank; all processing and storage functions are handled behind the scenes, while tellers, drive-up windows, and night deposit slots function as input and output devices.

Let's begin the tour by examining the system unit. If you have a PC at your disposal, you can remove the cover and look at the interior components. Be sure to follow the instructions for this procedure in the "Options" section of IBM's *Guide to Operations.* But first one tip: label the plugs and cables before you disconnect them. One way to do this is to color code them with stick-on dots. You can also buy printed adhesive labels for the back panel. Or you can make a sketch of the panel, labeling each port with the name of the peripheral that connects to it. If you don't have a PC or don't want to remove the system unit's cover, refer to Figure 1.2.

If you are standing in front of the open unit, what you see should look very similar to Figure 1.2. The metal enclosure on the upper right contains the power supply, with the power cord coming in from the back. Just to the cord's right is an outlet that can supply power to the IBM monochrome monitor, and to its left are louvers for the cooling fan. On the right side of the power supply is the on-off switch. Also notice the cables coming from the power supply's left side.

The computer's one or two disk drives (depending on the way your system is configured) are located in front of the power supply, occupying the lower right corner of the unit. (Very few PCs are used without disk drives. Most systems have either two floppy disk drives or one floppy disk drive and one hard disk drive.) If your PC has only one drive, it will be on the left side, and the area to its right will be empty. The XT has a floppy disk drive on the left and a large-capacity hard disk on the right. Power to operate the floppy disk drives, which spin at 300 revolutions per minute, comes from the cables just mentioned.

Plug-in board   *Motherboard*   *Power supply*

Figure 1.2A *The interior and back panel of a PC. Note that this PC has two floppy disk drives (bottom right and center). Openings for the PC's five expansion slots are visible on the right side of the back panel.*

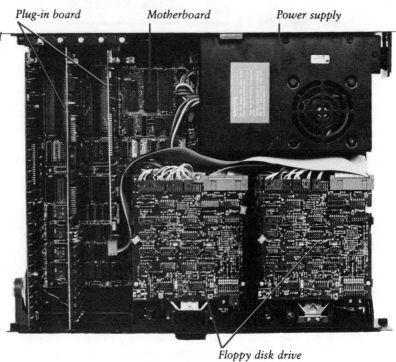

Floppy disk drive

Fan opening   *Expansion slot openings*

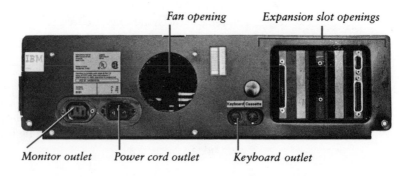

Monitor outlet   *Power cord outlet*   *Keyboard outlet*

Lying flat on the left half of the system unit is the *system board*. This is "the computer." It is a printed circuit board that holds the Intel 8088 microprocessor chip (the CPU) and a number of memory chips that give the 8088 something to work on. Avoid touching these chips, since even the miniscule amount of static electricity your finger may carry can damage them.

Notice that the memory is laid out in rows of nine chips each; eight of the chips are needed for storage of data, and the ninth is used to verify that data. Early PCs used 16K chips: one nine-chip row provided 16 *kilobytes* (K) of memory, enough to store 16,384

Figure 1.2B *The interior and back panel of an XT. Note that the XT has one floppy disk drive (bottom center) and a hard disk drive (bottom right). Openings for the XT's eight expansion slots are visible on the right side of the back panel.*

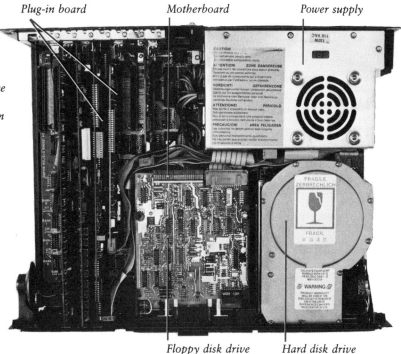

Plug-in board · Motherboard · Power supply

Floppy disk drive · Hard disk drive

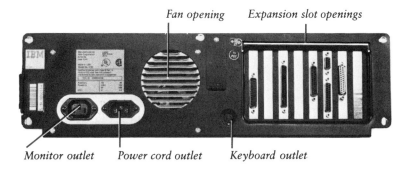

Fan opening · Expansion slot openings

Monitor outlet · Power cord outlet · Keyboard outlet

letters, numbers, or other characters. (One kilobyte equals 1024 bytes, or 2 to the tenth power.) Since mid-1983, IBM has been using 64K chips instead. Whereas the old board held 16K in one row, or 64K if all sockets on the board were full, the new board holds 64K per row, for a total capacity of 256K. A PC's board can have a single row of chips; or two, three, or all four rows can be filled. (After the first row, which is always provided by IBM, additional memory on the system board can be purchased with the machine or added later.)

The PC system board has five parallel *slots* (actually large sockets) that can hold additional, smaller boards or cards (the XT has eight such slots). These boards plug into the system board and get whatever power they need from it. Because this relationship is dependent, the system board is sometimes referred to as the *motherboard.*

These plug-in boards serve several purposes, one of which is to hold additional memory. Whether your motherboard contains 16K or 64K chips, plug-in boards can bring your machine's total memory capacity to as high as 640K (655,360 characters) or more. You may never need this much memory, but it's nice to have the option should the need arise. A typical PC today has about 128K of memory, though two to four times that is not uncommon. Increasingly, software designers are taking advantage of the PC's massive memory capacity. As this trend continues and memory becomes less expensive to purchase, we can expect more users to take advantage of the flexibility IBM built into the PC.

A second use of plug-in boards is to hold the circuitry that controls various components of the system. For example, one slot in the PC is occupied by a *controller* for the one or two floppy disk drives. The XT or a PC with a hard disk must also have a board that serves as a hard disk controller.

In addition, there must be an adapter board (the terms *card* and *board* are interchangeable) to link the computer to the monitor. IBM's design of the PC requires one board for the IBM monochrome monitor and another for color and graphics, but at least one other manufacturer offers a board that combines these capabilities.

Many other companies also make plug-in boards for the PC. Some of these boards duplicate IBM's, but many either provide additional functions or combine two or more functions on a single board. For example, many boards include a clock that can supply the time and date (which the PC requests whenever you turn it on). Some other special function boards are covered in Chapter 8.

The third purpose of plug-in boards is to link the PC to various external input and output (I/O) devices. This is done by means of the ports mentioned previously. Most printers require that data be sent to them through a *parallel port.* If your PC has the IBM monochrome monitor, the board that contains the display adapter also contains a parallel port. The IBM Color/Graphics Adapter does not include a printer port, however, so you'll need to use a separate slot for a printer port if you are using a color monitor.

Some printers require a *serial port,* sometimes called an *asynchronous port,* rather than a parallel port. Modems (for telephone communications) also require a serial port. You can buy the Asynchronous Communications Adapter from IBM for this purpose or a multifunction board that includes a serial port along with other components such as memory and a clock. If you want to use game controllers such as joysticks or paddles, you'll need a game adapter board. Whatever your needs, you can utilize the system board's slots to fit the PC or the XT to your particular requirements.

The Monitor

Every computer must have an input device for receiving instructions and data, a CPU, which processes the data according to the instructions, and an output device, which returns the processed material to the user. If the system unit, which contains the CPU, is the heart of the computer, the input and output devices are its extremities, its connections to the outside world.

The PC's basic output device is the monitor. The PC can also send output to other devices, including a printer, a modem, and, for more limited purposes, a speaker.

While the incredible power of personal computers sometimes makes us think they can do anything, even computers involve compromises. On the PC the monitor requires such a compromise. Monitor screens can display steady, highly detailed images, providing easy-to-read text. They can also display colorful, rapidly changing images, providing fast-moving animation. But the same monitor often cannot optimize both.

The image on the screen is transitory; if it is not continually recreated, or *refreshed,* it will disappear. For the highest quality flicker-free display, it is desirable that the image not begin to fade before it is refreshed. On the other hand, for fast-changing images such as animation, traditional television, or input from video disks, it is desirable that the residue of former images not linger while new ones appear. Thus, a manufacturer must choose to offer either one display mode that is adequate for both text and animation but optimizes neither, or two separate display modes. IBM chose the latter.

The PC's monochrome monitor is one of the best in the industry. It shows flicker-free, fully formed characters with serifs, true descenders (the bottom stems of the *y, g, p, j,* and *q* extend well below the other letters), and curves and diagonals that don't look more like staircases than parts of letters. The characters appear sharper than those on most other screens and have more space around them. But offering these features involves using a high-persistence phosphor display, which precludes effective animation. So video-style games are not feasible on the monochrome monitor.

You can have some graphics on a monochrome screen and text on a color screen, but there are trade-offs. Among color monitors, however, IBM's is one of the best. Chapter 8 covers this subject in greater detail.

Figure 1.3 *The keyboard supplied with the PC and XT. The central part of this keyboard is similar to that of a standard typewriter, with some extra keys added. In addition, the keyboard has ten function keys (on the left) and a numeric keypad (on the right).*

The Keyboard

Information can be sent to the computer from files stored on a disk, from a modem, or from a pointing device such as a mouse, which can be used with a number of programs for the PC and XT. If the monitor is the computer's basic output device, however, the keyboard is its basic input device.

The keyboard is probably the most personal aspect of a computer, because contact with it is tactile. Most people who have used the PC keyboard agree that it is one of the best on the market and that its solidity, curvature, finish, and tactile and auditory feedback make it a pleasure to use.

The keyboard's adjustable legs allow you to use it at either of two angles: an almost flat 5-degree angle, or a more slanted 15-degree angle. And the coiled connecting cable gives you freedom to move it at will. If you take the cord by both ends and stretch it out, it will be much looser and the keyboard easier to position.

The keyboard has one other feature that, while deceptively simple, is very convenient: a pencil ledge just above the top row of keys. As the name implies, you can set a pencil or pen on it. Depending upon the placement of your keyboard, you can also use it to prop up notes or documents. Two accessories are available that take advantage of the pencil ledge: templates that display often-used commands and function key definitions, and plastic dust covers.

As good as the PC's keyboard is, it does have at least two flaws. IBM has placed a few of the keys in nonstandard locations, which is a problem for touch typists. Because the <Shift> key is one place further to the left than on a standard typewriter, for example, *Henry* may come out *henry* or even \ \ *henry,* but most users adapt to the new locations quickly. And the <CapsLock>, <NumLock>, and <Ins> keys each act as a toggle: if it is off, pressing it turns it on; if on, pressing turns it off. Since the keys have no light or other status indicator, you may occasionally discover that you have typed a row of capital letters on the screen where you were expecting lowercase letters, or numbers when you merely wanted to move the cursor up or down a few lines.

Now let's look more closely at the PC's 83-key keyboard (see Figure 1.3). On the left are 10 function keys. On the right are 15 keys that make up the numeric keypad. The center portion of the keyboard, or the remaining 58 keys, is the typewriter area.

The white keys, except for a few extra symbols, are identical to those on most typewriters. All these keys, including the space bar, have an auto-repeat feature—the designated character will repeat for as long as you hold down its key.

The gray keys surrounding the letter, number, and symbol keys perform a variety of functions. Starting at the upper left, the <Esc> (escape) key will usually cause the computer to ignore whatever you have entered on the current line. With some programs it serves other functions (designated by the program). The key below it, with the left- and right-facing arrows, is the <Tab>. Pressing it moves the cursor to the next tab position to the right.

Next come <Ctrl> (control), <Shift> (two keys with upward-pointing arrows), and <Alt>. These keys do nothing by themselves and are used in conjunction with one or more other keys. You are probably familiar with shift keys from using a typewriter. Those on the PC work the same way, causing letters to shift to uppercase and other keys to display the upper of the two symbols shown on the keycaps. Additional commands can be sent to the computer by pressing <Ctrl> or <Alt> simultaneously with another key.

Above and to the right of the white typewriter keys is the <Backspace> key, designated by an arrow pointing to the left. Also called the "destructive backspace," it deletes the character to the left of the cursor and moves everything to the right of the deleted character one space to the left.

Below the <Backspace> key is <Enter>, symbolized by a bent arrow. With most programs, what you type appears on the screen but isn't actually entered into the computer until you press the <Enter> key. This process gives you a chance to check what you've typed and make any necessary changes in your data before the CPU acts upon it. Most word processing programs also use <Enter> to indicate the end of a paragraph.

Next is <PrtSc> (print screen). In lowercase mode it types an asterisk, but press it along with the <Shift> key, and (if your printer is turned on) whatever is on the screen will be printed on paper. If, instead of <Shift> you press <Ctrl>-<PrtSc>, the printer will "echo" the keyboard: whatever appears on the screen will also appear on paper until you press <Ctrl>-<PrtSc> a second time.

To the right of the space bar is <CapsLock>. Like the corresponding typewriter key, pressing <CapsLock> turns all letters into capitals. Unlike the typewriter version, however, pressing this key does not affect the number or punctuation keys. Also unlike a typewriter, pressing <Shift> on the PC does not release <CapsLock>; instead, you "toggle" off <CapsLock> by pressing it a second time. When <CapsLock> is on, however, pressing <Shift> generates lowercase letters.

The numeric keypad on the right serves two functions. Normally these keys (except <Numeric 5>) move the cursor around the screen. But if the <NumLock> key is toggled on, these keys provide an alternative way to enter numerical data that is generally much faster than using the top row of the keyboard. What if you are in the numeric mode and want to move the cursor? You do not have to press <NumLock>, move the cursor, and press <NumLock> a second time. Instead, hold down either <Shift> key, and the number pad will temporarily return to its cursor movement mode.

The four arrow keys move the cursor in the directions indicated by the arrows. In addition, when the cursor reaches the edge of the screen, it will generally *wrap around,* continuing forward to the beginning of the next line. When the cursor reaches the bottom line of the screen, pressing the <CursorDown> key moves the cursor down to yet one more line, which appears at the bottom of the screen, while the line previously at the top *scrolls* off the top of the screen. When the cursor reaches the last line of text, the <CursorDown> key has no further effect.

The <Home> key moves the cursor to the top-left position on the screen, and the <End> key moves it to the bottom left. With some programs the <PgUp> and <PgDn> keys are essentially page turners, scrolling up to show the previous screenful of data or down to the next. However, some programs do not implement these two keys.

Finally, we come to two of the most powerful keys on the keyboard. <Del> deletes the last character you entered, the one to the immediate left of the cursor. If you hold it down, it will keep moving to the left, deleting characters until you release it. Notice that it duplicates the action of the <Backspace> key. Pressing <Ins> allows you to insert new material. In the insert mode, if you type new material, the characters to the right of the cursor are pushed ahead to make room. Pressing <Ins> while in insert mode switches the keyboard back into strikeover mode. Consequently, anything you type will overwrite characters already on the screen.

The ten gray keys on the left side of the keyboard, marked <F1> through <F10>, are programmable function keys. Depending on the program you are using, they can take on almost any command or series of characters. If you are using BASIC, for example, <F3> loads a program into memory, and <F2> runs the program. The *WordStar* word processing program uses <F3> to set the left margin and <F2> to indent paragraphs, while <F9> and <F10> move the cursor to the beginning or the end of a file. Not only may each program define the function keys in its own way, but many programs allow you to redefine these keys to suit your needs.

The Printer

Although the system unit, the keyboard, and a monitor are all the computer needs to get its job done, you will probably need at least one more piece of hardware: a printer. Except for games and a few other applications, we usually want the end result of the computer's activity to be printed out on paper—*hard copy*—not just electronic copy.

All printers do basically the same thing: they take electronic information from the computer and transform it into the mechanical movement of a print wheel, a printhead, or another mechanism that puts letters and symbols on paper. But they don't all do this in the same way. One kind of printer uses a print wheel or a thimble that has individually formed characters much like a typewriter's. These letter quality printers provide high-quality printing and a wide range of interchangeable typefaces, but they are relatively slow and expensive. Dot matrix printers, which use a number of tiny wires in various combinations to create characters, are considerably faster and less expensive than letter quality printers, but their output is generally of lower quality. Dot matrix printers can, however, print high-resolution graphics. (For a detailed explanation of printers and their varying technologies, see *Hardware for the IBM PC and XT,* another book in the PC World Library.)

IBM does not manufacture its own printer for the PC. The IBM Graphics Printer is a slightly modified version of the Epson MX-80. The PC's letter quality printer is a specially configured NEC Spinwriter. Yet most other printers on the market, whether made by Epson, NEC, or some other manufacturer, can be used successfully with the PC. Usually, the only difficulty is cabling. Most dot matrix printers use a parallel connection, while letter quality printers use either a parallel or a serial connection. Regardless of the type of connection, each computer-printer combination requires a specialized cable. Since the PC is so popular, cables to connect it to most popular printers are readily available. Alternatively, a knowledgeable technician can construct a custom cable if your equipment requires it.

It is also possible to connect more than one printer to a single PC, by using two separate cables and connections, switching two cables between one connection on the PC, or attaching a special device to control two or more printers. You can use a dot matrix printer for graphics or to print rough drafts quickly and then switch to letter quality for business letters and final reports.

The Documentation

The components covered thus far in our tour are the major hardware items in a typical PC installation: the three essentials (system unit, monitor, and keyboard) plus a printer. Other hardware options can be added (we'll consider them in Chapter 8). But there is one essential component that we haven't examined—the manuals, or the *documentation*. Although the IBM manuals are certainly thorough, they are somewhat like Los Angeles freeways and New York subways: great once you understand them but confusing to newcomers.

The best way to take advantage of the manuals is to use them in three ways. First, browse through them. Familiarize yourself with what they cover, but don't worry about whether it makes sense yet. Don't panic at the abundance of material. Much of it you'll probably never need, and the rest you'll pick up in small increments, as necessary. In many ways, learning to use a computer is like learning to drive a car. At first, it may seem overwhelming, but after a while it all becomes second nature. Even though you can handle rush-hour traffic, follow complex directions, and carry on a conversation all at the same time, there are probably vast areas of automotive operation that are vague to you. But these gaps don't keep you from using your car. Thus, you don't need to memorize the PC's *Guide to Operations* any more than you had to memorize your car's manual.

Second (and this is what the IBM manuals seem to have been designed for), use them as a reference. When any specific question arises, look it up. You'll probably find exactly what you need, and since you have a specific need, the manual's explanation will probably make sense at that point.

Third, continue to peruse the manuals from time to time. Many points that didn't make sense the first time around will eventually become clear. Gradually, you'll become not only computer literate but computer competent, and—perhaps even more important —computer comfortable.

Essential Terms for PC and XT Users

BASIC   The computer language most widely used with microcomputers. A version of BASIC is supplied with the PC.

Bit   A short form of the words *binary digit,* this unit is either a 1 or a 0. The bit is the most elementary form of data in the computer; 8 bits make up 1 byte.

Board   The commonly used term for any printed circuit board that can be installed in one of the PC or XT expansion slots. (The terms *card* and *adapter* are also used to describe such a component.)

Boot   The process of loading the disk operating system into the computer.

Byte   One character of data used by the computer, such as a letter, a number, or a symbol. Each byte consists of 8 bits.

Column   The space occupied by one character on the computer screen. Most monitors used with the PC and the XT can display a line of text that is 80 columns (or characters) wide.

Command   An instruction to the computer, used in conjunction with a program, a language, or the disk operating system.

CPU   The central processing unit of a computer (also called the microprocessor), which performs the operations specified by commands.

Cursor   The location indicator on the computer screen. On the PC and the XT the cursor almost always takes the form of a blinking underscore symbol one character wide.

Disk   The principal data storage medium used by the PC and the XT. The floppy disk (called a diskette in the IBM manuals) used in standard systems is a removable mylar disk in a cardboard jacket that measures 5¼ inches in diameter. The XT also has a hard disk (called a fixed disk by IBM), a nonremovable 5¼-inch device that is sealed into its drive.

Disk drive   The device used to read and write data on floppy disks and hard disks. The disk drive contains a read/write head that moves back and forth over the spinning disk, rapidly depositing or locating magnetic signals that constitute the data to be written on the disk or already stored there.

Disk operating system (DOS)   The group of programs that control the flow of information into and out of the computer and manage data on disks. The most widely used DOS for the PC and the XT is PC-DOS.

File   A collection of data grouped together under one name for use within the computer's memory or for storage on a disk or other storage medium. Each separate document, program, budget, or other assemblage of information is a file, although many programs and collections of data consist of multiple files.

File name   The title given to each file, which can be up to 11 characters long (8 characters with a 3-character extension) for use with the PC and the XT. The file names are stored in the directory or subdirectories of disks and are used to locate the files.

Hardware   The physical components of a computer system.

Input   Data that is sent into the computer from any of several sources. The principal input device is the keyboard.

Kilobyte   Abbreviated K, this unit equals 1024 bytes.

Megabyte   Sometimes abbreviated M or Mb, this unit equals 1 million bytes.

Memory   The storage area for electronic data within the computer. The memory of the PC and XT consists of random access memory, or RAM, which is emptied each time the computer is turned off, and read-only memory, or ROM, which remains intact when the computer is turned off.

Menu A list of options displayed on screen as part of a program's operation.

Microprocessor Also known as the central processing unit, or *CPU*. The PC and the XT use the Intel 8088 microprocessor, a 16-bit microprocessor that can handle data in groups of 16 bits (2 bytes) at a time. An earlier generation of microcomputers used 8-bit microprocessors, such as the Intel 8080 or the Zilog Z-80, which process data in 8-bit groups and thus operate more slowly than 16-bit microprocessors.

Monitor The display unit of a computer system.

Motherboard The principal circuit board of the computer on which the micro-processor, the main memory, and other essential components are located.

Output Data that is sent from the computer to any of several devices, such as the monitor or a printer.

Peripherals Hardware devices that are not integral to the computer itself. The printer is a peripheral device, but disk drives are usually considered part of the computer.

Port A point within the computer for entry and exit of data. A printer is connected to the computer through one of the two types of ports: parallel or serial.

Program A set of instructions that has been specially formulated for computer use.

Prompt A symbol that appears on the computer screen to indicate that a program, a language, or an operating system is ready for use.

Software The collective term for programs.

System unit The component of the PC or the XT that contains the motherboard, expansion slots, and one or more disk drives.

Toggle A key that, when pressed, turns an operation on and off sequentially, such as the <CapsLock>, <NumLock>, and <Ins> keys on the PC and the XT.

CHAPTER TWO

Using the PC

● Remember the Bill Cosby routine about Noah and the Ark? God, played by Cosby (before George Burns got the role), told Noah, also played by Cosby, "I want you to build an ark."

And Noah replied, "Right! What's an ark?"

"Make it 40 cubits long."

"Right! What's a cubit?"

Your first sessions with the computer may seem similar. God, played by the documentation, says, "Format floppy disk, boot, and load program."

And you reply, "Right! What's a format?"

"Back up your disks."

"I didn't even know they could go forward."

Although the vocabulary of computing may seem alien at first, you'll quickly learn the requisite terms. And the most efficient way to learn is the way Noah probably did—by doing.

Most of the tasks in this chapter involve the PC and at least one floppy disk drive. If you have a PC with a hard disk (or fixed disk, as IBM calls it) or an XT, your system will also have a floppy disk drive, so you should be able to follow along. Chapters 8 and 9 focus on hard disks and the XT in more detail.

Getting Started
If your PC system is not set up, assembling it is a simple matter of following the instructions in the first section of the IBM *Guide to*

Operations. Putting together a PC is easier than assembling most night-before-Christmas children's toys. But do read the instructions first: an improperly connected plug may damage either the monitor or a part of the system unit.

Once you're ready to go, reach around to the right side of the system unit and flip up the red switch to the "on" position. After

```
The IBM Personal Computer BASIC
Version C1.00 copyright IBM Corp. 1981
62920 bytes free
Ok

_

1LIST 2RUN← 3LOAD" 4SAVE" 5CONT← 6, "LPT1 7TRON←8TROFF←9KEY 0SCREEN
```

Figure 2.1 *Screen display after Cassette BASIC has been loaded. The listing at the bottom of the screen shows the operation of each function key in BASIC.*

about six seconds you should see the *cursor,* a small blinking line, in the upper left corner of the screen. While the cursor is blinking, the PC is checking each of the memory chips as well as the internal circuits and whatever peripherals are hooked up. If your PC has 64K of memory, this process will take about 8 seconds; if you have more memory, you'll have to wait a little longer—about 23 seconds for a PC that has 256K, for example.

After your system checks itself out, the PC signals its completion with a single beep. Then the computer will look for a disk in drive A. If it doesn't find one, it will turn to a portion of memory called ROM for instructions. *ROM* stands for *read-only memory,* which means that its contents can be read but not changed. ROM contains several permanently installed programs, some of which run automatically every time you turn on the PC. These ROM-based programs do the testing mentioned above and then check to see if a disk is in one of the drives. If a disk is found, control is turned over to the disk-based programs. If there are no disk drives or if the drives are empty, another program located in ROM, Cassette BASIC, is loaded into memory. Cassette BASIC then prints a message on the screen like the one shown in Figure 2.1.

If your PC didn't beep once and display the lines shown in Figure 2.1 (although perhaps with different numbers), consult the "Problem Determination Procedures" section in the IBM *Guide to Operations.*

If you have an XT, you'll have to put the PC-DOS disk into the disk drive, then turn on the computer. Press <Enter> when you see questions about date and time; then you'll see the A prompt on the screen. Type **BASIC** and wait a few seconds, and you'll see a message similar to the one for Cassette BASIC on the PC.

A Brief Introduction to Programming

Contrary to what the name may imply, you don't need a cassette recorder to use the PC's version of Cassette BASIC. You would need a cassette recorder only if you wanted to use programs already stored on cassette or store programs that you write with this version of BASIC. The PC has two other versions of BASIC that permit programs to be saved on disks; these are discussed in Chapter 7.

BASIC enables the PC to follow fairly straightforward English instructions. Without BASIC or some other computer language, the PC would respond only to direct machine instructions—a series of 1's and 0's.

Let's try giving the computer some instructions. Type **HomeValue** = **86000.** You can use uppercase or lowercase letters; it doesn't matter. For numbers, use the top row of keys rather than the set on the right. Be sure not to substitute the letter O for the number 0, or the letter l for the number 1. If you make a mistake, use the <Backspace> key to correct it. If you want to erase the whole line, press <Esc> (escape).

It's important to realize two things when you use the computer keyboard. First, there is nothing you can do from the keyboard that will damage the computer. You can change or erase data or programs (which is why you'll be making backup copies of your disks), but you can't break anything. Second, the computer doesn't know what you're doing. In fact, the computer doesn't know anything. Not only aren't computers smart, they're not even dumb. A computer has no more intelligence than a microwave oven; it can do only what a person tells it to do. What's more, the computer doesn't keep track of what you are doing. Unless you are using an ultra-sophisticated accounting program that generates an audit trail, there is no way for a PC to monitor your activity, let alone make any judgments about it.

So relax, enjoy, and press a few more keys. In fact, if you didn't make any mistakes entering the first line, be sure to make a few in the next one so you can see how easy it is to correct them. Try pressing the <Backspace> and <Esc> keys.

When you have typed **HomeValue** = **8600** correctly, press <Enter>. The screen should then display 'Ok'. If your line has a mistake in it, you will see an error message on the screen. The most common error message is 'Syntax error', which means that what you've just typed might be good English, but it's not good BASIC. Simply retype the line correctly, press <Enter>, and you should be rewarded with the 'Ok', which is BASIC for "I've done what I should with your last entry and am ready for another."

Now type in three more lines, pressing <Enter> after each one.

```
CarValue = 8000 <Enter>
Furnishings = 5000 <Enter>
BankAccount = 100 <Enter>
```

Now that you've given the computer some information, you can tell it what the information means. Type

```
Assets = HomeValue + CarValue + Furnishings + BankAccount <Enter>
```

If you want to know the total value of the four items, you can simply ask by typing **Print Assets** <Enter>, and the screen will display '99100'.

While you're at it, type in the other side of the coin:

```
Mortgage = 53000 <Enter>
CarLoan = 4000 <Enter>
CreditUnionLoan = 2000 <Enter>
Liabilities = Mortgage + CarLoan + CreditUnionLoan <Enter>
```

To determine your total liabilities, type **Print Liabilities,** and the screen will display '59000'. Now that the PC has all this information, you can ask it to do whatever you want with it. Type

```
Print "Net Worth Is $" Assets - Liabilities <Enter>
```

If you put the quotation marks exactly where they are in the line above, the screen should display 'Net Worth Is $ 40100'.

All this effort won't eliminate the need for an accountant, but remember, you haven't even used the disk drives yet. What you did do, however, in just those few lines, was write your own program, enter some data, and run the program.

So far you've seen what the PC can do without any disks, using only the BASIC language built into the hardware. You've also gotten a taste of what programs are, how they work, and how they are written. But while the PC is an easy machine on which to develop programs, the range of commercially available programs is even more extraordinary. And since you'll probably be using prepackaged programs most of the time, let's turn to them.

A Brief Introduction to Programs

Most business applications of personal computers involve manipulating or communicating words, numbers, or other information. For processing words, obviously, you would use a word processing program. The most common kind of program for working with numbers is the *electronic spreadsheet,* a ledger-style calculation program, though various kinds of statistical analysis and accounting programs also fall into this category. A number of powerful data base management systems and simple filing programs are available for handling information. The work produced by these programs is usually either printed on paper or sent to another computer using a modem and a communications program.

Two additional kinds of programs are educational programs and utilities. While educational programs designed for children might seem like interactive versions of "Sesame Street" or *Pac-Man* with a purpose, a wide range of adult-level *computer-assisted instruction* (CAI) is also available. CAI can help you learn to operate your computer, learn a foreign language, take full advantage of a complicated program, or improve your typing.

Utilities are the software equivalent of an administrative assistant. Some utilities manage the computer's input and output and handle electronic files. Others can put a digital clock in the corner of your screen, send special instructions to your printer, or even recover files that have been accidentally erased.

All programs and data stored on disk must be used with a *disk operating system,* which is a collection of utilities that manage information within the computer and on the disks. The PC's disk operating system is introduced later in this chapter and discussed in detail in Chapters 3 and 10.

Using the IBM Diagnostics Disk: A Menu-Driven Program

Let's start by running a utility program that comes with the PC. In the back of the PC's *Guide to Operations* you'll find an envelope with a 5¼-inch floppy disk labeled Diagnostics. Keeping the disk in its paper envelope, remove it from the plastic pocket in the IBM binder. Disks hold an incredible amount of information, in easily accessible form, at a very low cost. Yet they can be damaged easily. Chapter 11 covers disk care in detail. For now just treat them gently, and follow the six basic rules printed on the back of the storage envelope.

You may see people disregarding these rules and apparently getting away with it, but such gambles are risky. If you lose valuable information even once, you will realize that a little effort can save a lot of data.

Now remove the Diagnostics disk from its envelope, slide it label side up into drive A (the one on the left), and close the drive's "door." Your screen probably still reads 'Net Worth Is $40100'. Recall that when we turned on the computer, it ran a power-on self-test to check its circuits, looked to see if a disk was in drive A, and then loaded Cassette BASIC from ROM into memory. That process is called *booting the system. Boot,* which is short for *bootstrap,* refers to the computer's getting itself started without your having to tell it what to do, akin to pulling itself up by its own bootstraps. To switch from the ROM-based Cassette BASIC to the disk operating system (DOS), you have to *reboot.*

One way to reboot is to turn off the computer, wait at least six seconds, and turn it back on. This is called a *cold boot.* The computer will find a disk in drive A and copy part of the disk's contents into the computer's main memory, where you will have ready access to it. A second way to reboot is called a *system reset* or a *warm boot*; this is done by holding down the <Ctrl> and <Alt> keys on the left side of the keyboard while pressing <Del> on the right. This two-handed, three-key procedure is deliberately clumsy to prevent accidental rebooting, which would erase whatever you had in memory at that point.

Let's take a brief look at the computer's main memory, also known as *RAM (random-access memory)*. RAM is simply the area that contains the material you are using at the moment, like the top of your desk. The disks are like file cabinet drawers. Material stored there can be brought to your desk, examined, changed, and refiled. There is an important difference, however. If a paper file is destroyed while it is out of the cabinet, that's the end of it. But when you read an electronic file from memory, the original is not touched because you are working with a copy. If you lose something from memory or want to ignore changes that you have made, you can go back and reread the original file from the disk.

When you have created something in RAM that you want to keep, you have to store it on a disk. Until you record it on disk, the information is only temporary; if a power failure occurs, if you turn off the machine, or if you do a system reset by pressing <Ctrl>-<Alt>-<Del>, the contents of RAM will be gone. Thus, IBM's two-handed system reset procedure minimizes the possibility of accidental erasure.

Getting back to our introduction to the Diagnostics disk, if your computer is already on, press <Ctrl>-<Alt>-<Del> simultaneously; if it is off, turn it on. The computer will beep, drive A will start operating, and the computer will load the operating system and the Diagnostics program. Loading simply means reading something from the disk (storage) into RAM (memory). When it finishes, your screen should look like Figure 2.2.

If you are using a version of DOS other than 2.00, the screen display will be slightly different (DOS 1.10 doesn't offer option 3, for example), but you should have no trouble following along.

You already have the Diagnostics disk in drive A, so type **0** <Enter>. The five-option menu shown in Figure 2.2 will be replaced by a listing of your particular PC's configuration: the amount of memory installed, the number of disk drives, the I/O (input/output) ports, and so forth. Below the list the screen will display 'Is the list correct (Y/N)? _'.

In this chapter you are running the Diagnostics routines to become familiar with operating the PC and running software, rather than to diagnose problems, so we will assume that your answer to

```
The IBM Personal Computer Diagnostics
Version 2.00 (C) Copyright IBM Corp. 1982, 1983

SELECT AN OPTION

0 - RUN DIAGNOSTIC ROUTINES
1 - FORMAT DISKETTE
2 - COPY DISKETTE
3 - PREPARE FIXED DISK FOR RELOCATION
9 - EXIT TO SYSTEM DISKETTE


ENTER THE ACTION DESIRED
? _
```

Figure 2.2 *The initial display when the Diagnostics disk is used with the PC or XT.*

```
SYSTEM CHECKOUT

0 - RUN TESTS ONE TIME
1 - RUN TESTS MULTIPLE TIMES
2 - LOG UTILITIES
9 - EXIT TO DIAGNOSTIC ROUTINES

ENTER THE ACTION DESIRED
? _
```

Figure 2.3 *Menu of options for System Checkout with the Diagnostics program.*

this question and those that follow is yes. If you uncover a problem, however, refer to the "Problem Determination Procedures" section in the IBM *Guide to Operations* or see Chapter 11.

Most programs, including this one, allow you to enter commands in either uppercase or lowercase letters. So type **Y** or **y** and press <Enter>. The configuration list will be replaced by the menu shown in Figure 2.3. Reply with **0** <**Enter**>, and pour yourself a cup of coffee. The screen will display the following message:

```
system unit     100
this test takes up to two minutes
please stand by
```

The actual time depends upon how much memory is installed in your PC, since at this point every chip, circuit, and device in your system unit is undergoing tests even more thorough than those done routinely when you first turn on the computer.

Once everything checks out, a new screen display will appear, showing five rows of small blocks in a pattern representing the keyboard. Press any letter on the keyboard. The corresponding block on the screen will be replaced with that letter. Try some number, punctuation, and other keys. Rather than releasing a key after you press it, hold it down for a few seconds. The character on the screen will flash on and off. You don't need to go through all 83 keys at this time. Try a few more, and then type **Y** <**Enter**> whenever you're ready.

The message 'keyboard 300' will appear for a moment at the bottom of the screen, and then the whole screen will be replaced by five lines, one at normal intensity, one intensified, one in reverse video, one blinking, and one underlined (a color monitor will not show underlining, however). Press **Y** <**Enter**> in response to 'Is the screen correct (Y/N)? _', and the lines will be replaced with the PC's full character set. Included are not only all the characters on the keyboard, but also foreign, scientific, and graphics characters. Below the display, the screen will again ask you to enter a Y or an N.

Enough of obeying the computer. What would happen if you didn't enter a Y or an N? Try it. The speaker in the system unit sounds a beep, and the computer waits for you to enter an acceptable choice. Earlier, when the menus were displayed, the computer would have responded to an improper entry by redisplaying the menu, with a new request for you to 'Enter the action desired'. Remember, you can't damage the computer from the keyboard, so relax, enjoy, and experiment.

At this point, you can remove the Diagnostics disk and either turn off the computer or put in another program and press <Ctrl>-<Alt>-<Del> to reboot. As a general rule, however, remove or swap disks under two conditions only: when a program you are running or a tutorial you are following says to, or when the last thing on the screen is the DOS prompt, an A (or possibly a B, a C, or a D) followed by an angle bracket (A>).

Using the DOS Disk: A Command-Driven Program

Like the Diagnostics routines that we just examined, the disk operating system (DOS) is a set of utility programs. Unlike the Diagnostics, however, which are used only when you set up, modify, or have problems with the PC, you will use DOS every time you use the computer. You even used it when you ran the Diagnostics program.

Although there are two disks labeled DOS in the back of the IBM *Disk Operating System* manual (only one if you have version

1.00 or 1.10), parts of DOS also reside on almost every disk you'll use with the PC. The complete PC-DOS is a set of more than two dozen programs. Some you may never use; others are so essential that you can't run an applications program without them. These essential parts of DOS are contained in the following three files: IBMBIO.COM, IBMDOS.COM, and COMMAND.COM. The Diagnostics disk contains both the Diagnostics program and these three files.

PC-DOS is the disk operating system sold most often with the PC and the XT. It is generally compatible with MS-DOS on many computers similar to the PC. Several other operating systems are available for the PC (including CP/M-86, Concurrent CP/M-86, the p-System, and various forms of UNIX), but PC-DOS is by far the dominant operating system.

Put the DOS disk in drive A (or in the only floppy drive of an XT or single-drive system), a blank disk in drive B, and turn on the computer or reboot (<Ctrl>-<Alt>-<Del>). No fancy lists of options this time, just a simple message:

```
Current date is Tue 1-01-1980
Enter new date:
```

If you enter the date according to the format IBM presents on the screen, it won't work: although the screen says 'Tue', the computer won't accept the day of the week. So just enter the appropriate numbers for the month, the day, and the year, separated by either slashes or hyphens, and then press <Enter>.

The new date will be entered, and the screen will ask for the time. Enter the hour followed by a colon, and then the number of minutes past the hour. The PC uses a 24-hour system: for 9:45 a.m., just enter 9:45; for 9:45 p.m., add 12 and enter 21:45. Too much hassle? You can skip the whole thing and just press <Enter> twice, once for the date and once for the time, and you won't have to enter any numbers at all. But it's a good idea to set the PC's internal clock whenever you turn on the machine, because it will label all your work with the proper date and time, which can come in handy later.

Now the screen will display the DOS A prompt (C if you have an XT). This tells you that DOS has been loaded into memory and awaits your command.

All applications programs are either *menu-driven, command-driven,* or a mixture of the two. The Diagnostics program was menu-driven: at each stage it presented you with a list of choices, and you made a selection from the menu, as you might in a restaurant. Now imagine a restaurant without menus. The waiter comes to your table (the gastronomic equivalent of the prompt), you request orange juice, coffee, two eggs over easy, and whole wheat toast. The waiter goes to the kitchen and eventually brings what you asked for.

Let's do the same with DOS. From the A prompt, type **FORMAT B:/S <Enter>**. That command directs DOS to format the disk in drive B, and the /S puts the "system" (the DOS files IBMBIO.COM, IBMDOS.COM, and COMMAND.COM) on the disk at the same time. The computer will respond with 'Insert new diskette for drive B: and strike any key when ready'.

Note that when you format a disk, you erase any information stored on it. So you must be extremely careful to designate the correct disk drive when using the FORMAT command. Always check to be sure that you've given a drive designator (A:, B:, and so on) and that the disk you want to format is in that drive. To be sure that you don't mistakenly erase data by formatting, you can check a disk's contents by typing the DIR (directory) command followed by the proper drive designator (such as DIR B:). If the disk has not been formatted, you'll get a disk error message.

If you have an XT, you must be especially careful when using the FORMAT command because it erases and reformats the hard disk as well as the floppy disks. The hard disk on the XT is designated as C (although you can change this to another letter using a different DOS command). So always be sure that you have not given the hard disk's letter as part of the FORMAT command. If you do not include a drive letter in the FORMAT command, drive C will be assumed, and you will erase all the data on the hard disk.

If you have a PC with only one disk drive, you can give the FORMAT command with no drive designator or with either A or B; both will allow you to swap disks to format with one drive. If you give no drive designator as part of your FORMAT command, DOS will assume that you're using the "default" drive, which is drive A on the PC and drive C (the hard disk) on the XT.

Notice that this time, rather than pointing to an item on a menu, you simply gave an instruction. As long as you type the command correctly, the machine will reply appropriately. Since you already have a new disk in drive B, press any key (or insert a blank disk if you're using an XT or a one-drive system). Drive B (the one on the right side) will start whirring, its red indicator light will glow, and the screen will announce what is happening: 'Formatting 9 sectors per track, 2 sides...'.

During the half-minute or so that this process takes, I will explain what formatting is. Visualize a large roll of paper, 8½ inches wide by hundreds of feet long. It provides a lot of space to write on but isn't very usable. First cut it into pieces 11 inches long, then put lines and page numbers on each sheet. You have just done the non-electronic equivalent of formatting a disk.

DOS 2.00 creates 40 concentric tracks on each side of a disk. (See Figure 2.4 for an illustration of a floppy disk.) At the same time, it does the electronic equivalent of drawing lines from the center to the edge, dividing each track into nine sectors. This creates a total of 360 sectors, each of which can hold 512 bytes (characters) of information. That's a grand total of 184,320 bytes per side, or 368,640 per disk if you have double-sided disk drives. Since 1K is 1024 bytes, that works out to 360K. A single-sided disk drive can store information on only one side of a disk, for a total of 180K if the disk is formatted with DOS 2.00.

DOS 1.10 or 1.00 also creates a 40-track disk, but with only eight sectors, so a disk formatted with 1.10 has a capacity of 40 tracks by eight sectors by 512 bytes, or 163,840 bytes per side. A double-sided disk formatted under DOS 1.10 has a capacity of 327,680, or 320K bytes. DOS 2.00 checks each disk to see how it is formatted and can read eight- and nine-sector disks with equal ease. But DOS 1.10 can read only eight-sector disks, so you cannot read disks formatted with DOS 2.00 when you are using DOS 1.10. That's one reason we've emphasized the use of DOS 2.00 throughout this book.

By now your computer should have finished formatting the disk and transferring the operating system. The screen will now look like this:

```
A>FORMAT/S B:

Insert new diskette for drive B:
and strike any key when ready

Formatting...Format complete
System transferred

      362496 bytes total disk space
      40960 bytes used by system
      321536 bytes available on disk

Format another (Y/N)? _
```

Press N, and you're back to the A prompt. Now that you have a formatted disk, you can store information on it. One way is to create

Figure 2.4 *A 5¼-inch floppy disk.*

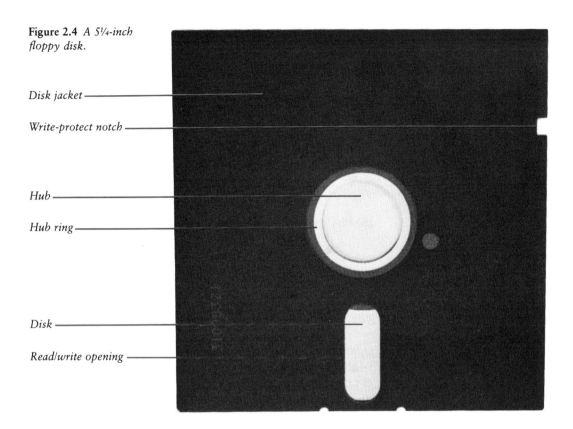

Disk jacket —————

Write-protect notch —————

Hub —————

Hub ring —————

Disk —————

Read/write opening —————

the information yourself, at the keyboard. You'll do this when you use the computer for word processing. Another way is to copy already-existing information—programs or data—to the disk from another disk. Again, remember that this is like making a photocopy, not like physically carrying a file from one file cabinet to another. You make a duplicate, and the original remains filed, undisturbed.

Type **DIR B**: <**Enter**> to get a directory of the disk in drive B (Figure 2.5), or simply **DIR** if you have only one drive. As usual, you can use uppercase or lowercase letters, or both.

The system, which you transferred to this disk while you were formatting, contains three files. The directory shows only one: COMMAND.COM. The other two, IBMBIO.COM and IBMDOS. COM, are hidden files: they are not listed in the directory, and you can't get at them the way you can access your own files. You can't read them (which is not a problem since you will have no need to), and you can't write to them, which protects them against accidental changes that would interfere with their functioning. They just sit there, out of sight, and make your whole system work.

```
A>DIR B:

Volume in drive B has no label
Directory of B: \

COMMAND    COM    17664      3-08-83   12:00p
               1 file(s)           322304 bytes free

A> _
```

Figure 2.5 *The directory of the disk in drive B.*

IBMBIO stands for IBM basic input/output, and IBMDOS stands for the IBM Disk Operating System. These two files are like traffic cops, directing the flow of electronic data to and from the keyboard, the monitor, the printer, and whatever other peripherals you may use. These files are the core of DOS and control the disk drives when they store or retrieve information from the floppy disks. COMMAND.COM is what prints the DOS prompt and interprets and executes the commands you enter from the keyboard. It contains the DIR program (which you just used) as well as COPY, TYPE, TIME, and several more, which you will have a chance to use in the next chapter.

The directory gives the date and time at which each file was last updated, and at the bottom of the list shows the number of files and the amount of unused space on the disk.

Now type **DIR A:** <**Enter**> to get a directory of the disk in drive A (you could just type **DIR** if the A prompt is showing). The format of this directory is the same as that of the previous one, but because the display is too large to fit on the screen, the top lines have scrolled off the top. There are two ways to make sure you can read the whole directory. One is to add /P (for pause) to your request: **DIR A:/P** <**Enter**>. Try it. The two title lines still scroll off, but you won't lose any file names. Notice that in addition to COMMAND.COM and the two hidden files, drive A contains 22 files. (You will use some of these in the next chapter.) Press any key, and the rest of the display will scroll onto the screen. There are just a few more lines, but on some disks you could have a directory that takes up two or three full screens.

Instead of adding /P you can add /W for wide. This time, instead of a single column, the directory will display the file names five across, but without the additional information about each one. Try it: **DIR A:/W** <**Enter**>.

You're probably getting tired of reading directories at this point, so remove the disks and turn off the computer. You will be using the newly formatted disk later, so label it before putting it away. Because the pressure from a pencil or ball-point pen can damage the disk, either fill out the label before attaching it or use a felt-tip pen whenever you write on the disk label.

Let's review your current computer capabilities. You now have a bit of programming experience. Although you aren't ready to develop your own program, you should understand what writing one would entail. You are also able to operate both menu-driven and command-driven programs. Your experience with command-driven programs includes the ability to use some of the most essential DOS commands.

Not too long ago, you had to be a programmer to be computer literate. Today, with the wide availability of off-the-shelf software, that definition is obsolete. You may not be an expert yet, but consider yourself computer literate. And if you are not quite computer comfortable, you are well on the way.

CHAPTER THREE

Using PC-DOS

As noted in the previous chapter, the disk operating system, PC-DOS, is a collection of utilities that manage data in the computer system. DOS can also make backup copies of disks and files, display the contents of a file on the screen, indicate the amount of space available in memory, and erase files. If you erase a file and later decide that you should have kept it, DOS can even—under certain conditions—recover it. And that's just the beginning.

DOS recognizes more than 40 different commands. It also contains some complete programs, including EDLIN, DEBUG, and LINK, that have their own sets of commands. Many of these more complex features of DOS are intended for programmers or advanced users. You probably will never need more than a dozen DOS commands, and you can learn these essentials in an hour or so.

In Chapter 2 you learned that two of the three basic DOS files, IBMBIO.COM and IBMDOS.COM, are hidden and are not listed in the directory. These two files always stay behind the scenes and do their work without your being aware of their presence. In computer parlance, they are *transparent*. The rest of DOS resides in COMMAND.COM and various other *user files*, ready to go into action upon request.

Most applications programs do their best to make all of DOS transparent. They do this by having their own commands, often in menu form, to activate DOS. Consequently, PC owners can use their computers without having to learn much about DOS. It is even possible to use the PC without being aware of DOS's existence—possible, but not advisable.

Why should you learn how to use DOS if your applications programs do everything for you? That's like asking why you should learn to set the shutter speed and lens opening on your camera when you could just set it on automatic. For average pictures in average situations, you could do just that, but to get the best results, maximize control and flexibility, and have the ability to handle unexpected problems, you have to assume control. The same idea applies to using the PC or the XT.

Understanding DOS

If you understand four basic concepts about DOS, using it will be easy: internal and external commands, file specification, the structure of DOS commands, and default disk drives.

Internal and external commands   In Chapter 2 you learned that when the computer "loads" a program, it copies the program into memory (RAM) so you can use it. Recall that this is a copy; DOS never removes the original from the disk unless you give it the ERASE command (or DEL, for delete). When you turn on the PC with a disk in drive A, you are loading DOS. If you are loading another program, the computer normally loads DOS at the same time but might keep it transparent, not even displaying the DOS A prompt (A>). Many programs display their own prompt, such as 'Ok' (BASIC), '*' (EDLIN), '-' (DEBUG), '.' (*dBASE II*), or just the flashing cursor (most word processing programs). Regardless of whether you can see evidence of DOS's presence, it's always there.

It would waste space to keep all of DOS in memory, so when you load DOS, only the most often-used parts of it go into memory. Therefore, when you type a command such as FORMAT, DOS has to go back to the disk for it. The parts of DOS that reside in memory are called *internal commands*; those that reside on disk but are in memory while they are being used are called *external commands*.

Once you have loaded DOS, you can remove the DOS disk, perhaps replacing it with a program disk, and all the internal commands will still be accessible. You will be able to execute an external command, however, only if you replace the DOS disk or have copied the file that holds the desired command (such as FORMAT) onto the disk you are using.

File specification   While some DOS utilities (such as FORMAT) work on the disk as a whole, most of the DOS commands operate on individual files. Electronic files are similar to paper filing systems in several respects. A disk is the equivalent of a file drawer; the mass of information on a disk or in a file drawer is organized into files, and each file is labeled with a name. File folders have a tab with a letter, a word, or a few words identifying their contents, such as "MARKETING PLAN, WIDGETS"; electronic files have a file specification, or *filespec,* such as MKTPLAN.WGT. If you want to read or modify the Widget marketing plan, DOS will serve as a highly efficient file clerk; it will go to the disk, make a copy of MKTPLAN.WGT, and put the copy in memory so you can work with it at any time.

The computer's memory (RAM) is essentially an electronic equivalent of your desktop. Perhaps consciousness would have been a better name than memory, since, unlike human memory, RAM is always immediately accessible. Although computer scientists might wince at this idea, I think of memory as an area just behind the PC screen, and the screen as a window that lets me look at a portion of whatever is in that area. To remind myself of the volatility of memory, I think of the information as floating in an electronic never-never land; it has no permanence until I instruct DOS to save it on disk.

The first part of the filespec, MKTPLAN, is called the file name. The second part, .WGT, is called the extension, sometimes abbreviated ext. The file name can be up to eight characters or spaces long, and can contain almost any combination of letters and numbers as well as certain punctuation marks. (Many people use *file name* rather than *filespec* to describe the complete name and extension.)

A file needn't have an extension; a file name alone is sufficient. But extensions can often provide useful information about a file's contents. Some extensions have standard meanings: .BAS signifies a program written in BASIC, .TXT designates a file containing text rather than a program, and .BAT indicates a batch file, a series of commands that DOS executes sequentially. You can also make up your own extensions, such as .LET for letters or .614 for a file created on June 14. Some additional tips on using file names and extensions are presented in Chapter 4.

Command structure While the various DOS commands serve different purposes, they share a common pattern that makes them easy to use. Let's say you have a disk that holds records for your company's New York branch. You want to transfer one file, CURINVNT (for current inventory), to a disk that contains inventory records for all the other branches. You could use the DOS command COPY A:CURINVNT B:. This command tells DOS to locate a file named CURINVNT on drive A and copy it to the disk in drive B. (If you have a one-drive system, this command will still work; simply change disks when the message on the screen prompts you to do so.) You can also copy a file and give the copy a different name from the original. For example, the command COPY A:CUR-INVNT B:NYBRANCH would rename the current inventory file on drive B to reflect its New York contents.

Notice that DOS expects the same address layout as the post office: the originator's address on the left and the recipient's address on the right. If you told DOS to COPY B:CURINVNT A:NY-BRANCH, it would look for CURINVNT on drive B, and if it found that file, it would place a copy with the title NYBRANCH on drive A. If DOS could not find CURINVNT on drive B, it would respond with the message 'File B:CURINVNT not found'.

Default drives   The A prompt tells you that your current drive is A. Another name for the current drive is the default drive; if you don't specify which drive DOS should go to, it goes to the current drive by default. (In both the PC and the XT, drive A is the initial default drive; when you turn on or reboot the computer, drive A is activated, and the part of DOS called the system is loaded from the disk in drive A into memory. If drive A lacks a disk or the system is not on the disk in that drive, you must insert a system disk in drive A before you can use DOS. In the XT, however, if drive A lacks a system disk, control is transferred to the hard disk, drive C, and it becomes the default drive.)

The default principle also applies to file names and other operations. When you were copying, for example, you could have left out the first drive designator and typed the command **COPY CURINVNT B:NYBRANCH**. DOS would still have gone to A for both the command and the file. You could also have typed **COPY CURINVNT B:**. In this case, you didn't specify a new file name, so by default the old name was used.

What if you shortened the command still further by leaving off the B:? DOS would again default to drive A, thinking that that is where you wanted the file copied. But instead of making the copy, it would tell us, 'File cannot be copied onto itself'. But as long as you give the copy a different name from the original, it will accept the command. An example might look like this: **COPY CURINVNT NYBRANCH**. Now you will have two copies of this file on the disk in drive A, one named CURINVNT and another NYBRANCH.

You should now have a good feel for the way DOS commands work. First, right after the DOS prompt, you type the name of the command preceded by the drive designator if the command isn't an internal command or on the drive indicated by the prompt. Some commands, such as FORMAT and DIR, operate on one disk or file at a time. With these you can leave off the drive designator if what you are doing involves the default drive. Otherwise, include the drive designator. Other commands, such as COPY, involve material on two drives or two files on the same drive. In either case, the original location, or *source,* goes on the left, and the new location, or *target,* on the right.

Using DOS Commands

Now let's go through some of the other DOS commands. Put the DOS disk in drive A and the disk you formatted in drive B so you can follow along.

CHKDSK   We'll start with CHKDSK. Pronounced "check disk," it does just what its name implies: it checks a disk and reports, in more detail than DIR, how much space is available for storing programs or data.

Try it. Type **CHKDSK** <Enter>. Since we didn't designate a drive, DOS automatically goes to the default drive—the one whose letter appeared in the prompt. Since that letter was an A, you got a readout on drive A. Try it again, this time watching your disk drives. The red indicator light on drive A goes on, and you can hear the drive operating.

The original DOS disk in drive A is formatted on just one side, allowing it to be used in both single- and double-sided drives, so it starts out with 180K. Since 4.5K are used internally, that leaves 175.5K, the 179,712 shown in Figure 3.1.

You can also check drive B by typing **CHKDSK B**: <Enter>. This time drive A will operate first, as DOS loads the external CHKDSK command into memory, and then drive B, as CHKDSK examines its contents.

Except for the numbers, which may be different, your screen should now match Figure 3.1. The total capacity of the double-sided disk in drive B is 360K, but since 6K is devoted to an internal directory and other housekeeping tasks, the total usable disk space is 354K times 1024 bytes per K, or 362,496 bytes. The hidden files are IBMBIO.COM and IBMDOS.COM, two of the three DOS system files. Notice that your newly formatted disk on drive B has only one user file. The file is COMMAND.COM, the third of the three DOS system files placed on the disk when you used the /S option with the FORMAT command. The bottom two lines of each message indicate the total amount of RAM and the amount currently available.

Occasionally, a disk will have a bad sector. When you use the FORMAT command, DOS tests the disk for bad sectors; if it finds

```
A>CHKDSK

 179712 bytes total disk space
  22016 bytes in 2 hidden files
 126464 bytes in 23 user files
  31232 bytes available on disk

 262144 bytes total memory
 237352 bytes free


A>CHKDSK B:

 362496 bytes total disk space
  22016 bytes in 2 hidden files
  17664 bytes in 1 user file
 322816 bytes available on disk

 262144 bytes total memory
 237352 bytes free


A> _
```

Figure 3.1 *A display of the results of the CHKDSK command for disks in drive A (top) and drive B (bottom). Note that CHKDSK reports the disk content and memory use within the computer.*

any, it marks them off so that no attempt will later be made to store data on them. If any bad sectors have been found, CHKDSK will report that as well.

COPY   So far you have used DIR, CHKDSK, and FORMAT. You have also learned about the COPY command but haven't actually used it. Let's do so now. You should still have the DOS disk in drive A and a formatted disk in drive B. Request a wide directory of the contents of drive B by typing **DIR B:/W** <**Enter**> (in a one-drive system you'll have to switch disks after giving that command). Drive B contains only one user file, COMMAND.COM. Now get a wide directory of drive A. Since A is the current (default) drive, you can simply type **DIR/W** <**Enter**>. If you are using an XT, you may be in the hard disk, so you'll get a very long directory. One advantage of the /W option is that it usually allows you to compare two directories on one screen (except when one is of a hard disk).

Let's copy some files from drive A to drive B. For the first one type the complete form of the command: **COPY A:FORMAT.COM B:FOR-MAT.COM** <**Enter**>. The file name and extension will appear on the screen, drive A will light up and whir, then drive B will do the same thing, and the message '1 File(s) copied' will appear on the screen. Finally the A prompt will reappear. When the prompt reappears after you have entered a command, you know that the computer has taken action; either the command has been completed, or the screen will display a message of explanation.

Now copy CHKDSK. Type **COPY A:CHKDSK B:CHKDSK** <**Enter**>. You will see 'A: CHKDSK File not found 0 file(s) copied' on the screen followed by the A prompt.

What's wrong? The first thing to check is the spelling. COPY and CHKDSK are both spelled correctly. Let's look at the directory again. **DIR/W** <**Enter**>. Aha, we left out the extension. While a filespec can consist of a file name without an extension, if it has an extension, you must include it when issuing a DOS command. Try again: **COPY A:CHKDSK.COM B:CHKDSK.COM** <**Enter**>. This time you will see 'CHKDSK.COM' followed by the A prompt.

Now copy DISKCOPY onto drive B. Since you are retaining the same filespec, there is no need to repeat it. So this time leave the second file name and extension off, and DOS will, by default, give the new file the same name as the old. Type **COPY A:DISKCOPY.COM B:** <**Enter**>. You will see 'DISKCOPY.COM' on the screen followed by the A prompt.

Now copy DISKCOMP. Although you have been telling DOS to get the file being copied from drive A, since that is the default drive you can leave off the drive designator: **COPY DISKCOMP.COM B:** <**Enter**>. You will see 'DISKCOMP.COM' on the screen followed by the A prompt.

Finally, copy the COMP file. Use whichever form you wish. DOS should reply with the filespec COMP.COM followed by the A prompt.

To make sure everything transferred the way you wanted, ask for a directory of B. This time use DIR without the /W. Your screen should look like Figure 3.2.

The files are all there, including the size of each one and the date and the time—not of this transfer but of their creation or last change. Neither COPY nor DISKCOPY (which you will use shortly) changes the time or date message. The disk's original capacity has been reduced by the space required for these six files, the two hidden files, and a few behind-the-scenes housekeeping tasks, but over 300,000 bytes are still available—the equivalent of two-thirds of this book.

Up to now, A has been the default drive. To change it to B, simply type **B:** <**Enter**>, and the B prompt will appear. Enter a few DIR and CHKDSK commands, with and without drive designators.

```
A>DIR B:

Volume in drive B has no label
Directory of B:

COMMAND COM   17664   3-08-83        12:00p
FORMAT    COM    6016   3-08-83        12:00p
CHKDSK    COM    6400   3-08-83        12:00p
DISKCOPY  COM    2444   3-08-83        12:00p
DISKCOMP  COM    2074   3-08-83        12:00p
COMP      COM    2523   3-08-83        12:00p
           6 file(s)         303359 bytes free

A> _
```

Figure 3.2 *The directory of the disk in drive B after copying of designated files.*

Change back to drive A and do the same thing. Now remove your original DOS disk, put it in its envelope, put it away, and switch the new disk to drive A. Again experiment with DIR and CHKDSK. Notice that if you ask for something on the now-empty B drive (if you have a second drive), DOS will look there and report:

```
Not ready error reading drive B
Abort, Retry, Ignore? _
```

You can just type A for abort, and the B prompt will reappear. Also try typing R or I, and see what happens.

DISKCOPY   So far, you have copied files one at a time. The DISKCOPY command copies a whole disk at once. And if the target disk hasn't been formatted, DISKCOPY will format it at the same time. Type **DISKCOPY A: B:** <Enter>. (When issuing a command, you need only type the name of the command, not the extension.) The screen will ask you to put the source disk in A, the target disk in B, and strike any key when ready. *Any* means any character key, not a function key or the <Ctrl> key—but don't do it yet. Like FORMAT, DISKCOPY erases everything on the target disk before copying the contents of the source disk to it. So using DISKCOPY with a target disk that contains important programs and information can be disastrous. Use DISKCOPY to make backup copies of entire disks, using only a blank disk as the target. To add files to a disk that already contains information you want to keep, use the COPY command.

41   *Using PC-DOS*

The surest way to guard against accidentally erasing data is to take advantage of the *write-protect* feature. Most 5¼-inch floppy disks have a small rectangular cutout on one side. As long as the cutout is exposed, a drive can add or delete information. Each box of disks, however, comes with a sheet of adhesive labels that can be used to cover this cutout. As long as one of these tabs is on the disk, data cannot be added or erased. Some disks that should never be written to, including the original PC-DOS and Diagnostics disks, do not have the cutout, so you cannot alter their contents.

Now copy the original DOS disk in drive A by putting a blank, unformatted disk in drive B and striking a key. The screen will tell you that the computer is copying and formatting at the same time. When it finishes it will ask if you want to copy another disk. Press N, and you will see the A prompt again. Remove the original DOS disk from drive A and put it safely away; then take the copy of DOS out of drive B and put it in drive A. Next, place the practice disk you previously used in drive B back in that drive. Then do another DISKCOPY operation (**DISKCOPY A: B:** <Enter>), so that you have DOS disks in both drives.

DISKCOMP Both the DISKCOPY and COPY procedures are usually error-free, but if you are backing up critical disks or files, "usually" may not be good enough. If you type **DISKCOMP A: B:** <Enter>, DOS will compare the two disks to make sure every sector is identical.

COMP You can also compare individual files. If you type **COMP A:CHKDSK.COM B:CHKDSK.COM** <Enter>, DOS will first make sure that the files are the same size (if they aren't, it will stop and tell you) and will then compare them sector by sector. As you might have guessed, you could have shortened this command to COMP A:CHKDSK.COM B: or interchanged the A and B designators. To see what happens if the files differ, type **COMP A:CHKDSK.COM B:DISKCOMP.COM** <Enter>.

An alternative to using COMP is verifying the COPY procedure as you execute it. To verify, simply add /V at the end of a COPY command after the second filespec. COMP (or DISKCOMP) might still be used at another time, not to confirm the accuracy of a COPY, but to see if two files are really the same.

CLS You have now used all the external commands on your disk but only two internal ones: DIR and COPY. Let's try a few more internal commands. Here's an easy one: CLS <Enter>. Any time the clutter on the screen is either confusing or merely unaesthetic, ask DOS to clear the screen with CLS. The command affects only the screen, not anything in memory or on a disk.

```
A>B:CHKDSK A:

363496 bytes total disk space
 22016 bytes in 2 hidden files
 28647 bytes in 4 user files
312833 bytes available on disk

262144 bytes total memory
237352 bytes free

A> _
```

Figure 3.3 *An example of using the CHKDSK command from a drive that is not the logged drive.*

ERASE ERASE or DEL does to a whole file what CLS does to the screen. Use it gingerly. Let's say you need more space on the disk in drive A, and you don't expect to need the CHKDSK command. Type **ERASE CHKDSK.COM** <Enter>. The computer responds with:

```
Write protect error writing drive A
Abort, Retry, Ignore? _
```

Open drive A, remove the disk, and take off the write-protect label; then reinsert the disk and press R. Drive A will go into action, and then the A prompt will come up again. Ask for a directory of A. Your other five files are still there, but CHKDSK.COM is gone, and your bytes free have increased by the 6400 that CHKDSK occupied.

Let's also get rid of the DISKCOMP command. You can type ERASE again or DEL: **DEL DISKCOMP.COM** <Enter>. Confirm with a directory, a wide one this time (DIR/W). Underneath let's run a check disk: **CHKDSK** <Enter>. Since you erased CHKDSK, DOS chides you for entering a 'bad command or filename'. You have a copy of CHKDSK on drive B, however, so while still logged onto drive A, have DOS go to B for CHKDSK and apply it to the disk in drive A (see Figure 3.3 for an example).

You could accomplish the same thing by first changing the default drive to B, then typing CHKDSK without the drive designators, as follows:

B:<Enter>
CHKDSK <Enter>

Typing **A**: will put you back on drive A.

So far you have used FORMAT, DISKCOPY, DISKCOMP, COPY, COMP, ERASE, CHKDSK, CLS, and the three versions of DIR (DIR, DIR/P, and DIR/W). Using these commands, you have formatted disks, copied entire disks and individual files, compared disks and files, determined contents, and deleted files. Two additional DOS commands will also be very useful in handling files; these are TYPE and RENAME.

TYPE   The TYPE command allows you to display the contents of most text files on the screen. Some programs store files in a condensed form, so you may not be able to view them with the TYPE command, and the contents of most programs cannot be displayed with TYPE. If you try to view a program or file that can't be displayed, you'll generally get some odd characters on the screen, and possibly some readable text as well.

Try the TYPE command with one or two of the files on the DOS disk. Because this disk contains all program files, you will not be able to view a plain text file. Try to view the FORMAT program by typing **TYPE FORMAT.COM**. Not all programs produce such noisy results as FORMAT; try MUSIC.BAS (a BASIC program) by typing **TYPE MUSIC.BAS**. To stop the text display temporarily, press <Ctrl>-<NumLock>; to restart the display, press any key. To stop the display and return to the A prompt, press <Ctrl>-<Break>.

Although you can't get much information from viewing these programs, you will find the TYPE command helpful when you have several text files on a disk and are not sure which one you want to use. A quick look with TYPE can usually tell you.

RENAME   Finally, let's rename a file. You may have modified the file so much that its original name is no longer appropriate, or the disk might now contain additional files with similar content, and you need to differentiate among them. Or maybe you have just decided that the original name can be improved. Let's change the name FORMAT to PREPDISK. (Normally, you would change only the names of the files you have created, not DOS files.) The command structure is the same as you are used to: source on the left, target on the right. Type **RENAME FORMAT.COM PREPDISK.COM** <Enter>. Confirm the result by viewing the disk directory.

Rather than typing RENAME in full, you can shorten it to REN. Switch the file back to its original name with **REN PREPDISK.COM FORMAT.COM** <Enter>. Again, a directory will confirm the change.

You have now learned 11 DOS commands. For most purposes, they are all you will need. The next chapter will show you how to use them to organize and keep track of the various programs and information files you will be accumulating. Along with these commands, you will learn a few more operations that, while not absolutely essential, can be very helpful.

Tips for Using DOS

■ Although a disk must be formatted before it can be used, you have to format a disk only once. When a disk is reformatted, any information on it will be lost.

■ If you have a single-drive system, you will probably always want to use the /S option with the FORMAT command so that you can use any disk to boot the operating system.

■ If you know part of the file name of files you are trying to find, use the '*' and '?' characters in conjunction with the DIR command to locate them.

■ Whenever the computer writes data to a disk, it is a good idea to verify that no errors have been made. You can use the /V option with the COPY command and the COMP and DISKCOMP commands. The simplest method of verifying, however, is to put a VERIFY ON statement in an AUTOEXEC.BAT file so that all data written to the disk will be checked.

■ Always make backup copies of important data and programs. It is too easy to erase a file accidentally or misplace a disk.

■ Label all disks clearly (using a felt-tip pen, not a ball-point pen or pencil). Labeling can save a great deal of time in locating a specific file.

■ Use meaningful file names and the same extensions for related files. Make a list of the file names and extensions you use repeatedly, and keep a copy near the computer for reference.

Essential DOS Commands

Command	Purpose	Example	Result
FORMAT	To prepare a disk for storage of data	FORMAT B:/S	Disk in drive B is formatted and system files are placed on the disk.
		FORMAT /1	Disk in the logged drive is formatted on one side only.
DIR	To display the contents of a disk	DIR B:	Display main directory of drive B.
		DIR *.BAS	Display all files on the logged drive that have the extension .BAS.
		DIR /W /P	Display current directory in wide format (/W) and pause (/P) after each screenful.
DISKCOPY	To copy the contents of one disk onto another	DISKCOPY A: B:	Make a copy of disk A onto disk B.
		DISKCOPY /1	Copy one side of the disk in the logged drive onto another disk using the same drive (swap disks).
DISKCOMP	To compare two disks	DISKCOMP A: B:	Compare disk A to disk B.
		DISCOMP /1	Compare one side of two disks on the logged drive (swap disks).

Command	Purpose	Example	Result
COPY	To copy a file	COPY DATA B:	Copy DATA from the logged drive to drive B.
		COPY DATA INFO /V	Make a copy of DATA called INFO on the same drive and verify (/V) that there are no errors.
COMP	To compare files	COMP FILE1 B:	Compare FILE1 on the logged drive to FILE1 on drive B.
		COMP *.BAS *.BAK	Compare all files with extension .BAS on the logged drive with all files with extension .BAK on the same drive.
ERASE **(DEL)**	To erase file(s) from a disk	ERASE MYFILE DEL *.*	Erase MYFILE from the logged drive. Remove all files from the current directory.
RENAME **(REN)**	To change the name of a file	RENAME ASDF QWER REN *.TXT *.BAK	Change the name of file ASDF to QWER. Change the extensions of all file names ending in TXT to end in .BAK.
CHKDSK	To produce a status report of a disk showing free space and to fix	CHKDSK	Status report of the logged disk is displayed.
		CHKDSK /F /V	As CHKDSK prepares a status report, detailed messages are displayed (/V), and any errors found in the directories will be corrected (/F).
TYPE	To display the contents of a file	TYPE MYFILE	Display MYFILE on the screen.
VERIFY	To verify that data written to a disk has been correctly recorded	VERIFY ON	After writing any data to the disk, the computer will check to see whether an error has been made.
		VERIFY OFF	Disable this feature.
PRINT	To print as many as ten files while the computer performs other tasks	PRINT MYFILE FILE1 PRINT FILE1 /C	Print MYFILE and FILE1 on printer. Cancels printing of FILE1.

CHAPTER FOUR

Electronic Filing

Although you may never be able to determine how many angels could dance on the head of a pin, figuring out how much information could be stored there is a bit easier. A pinhead-sized portion of a floppy disk can hold approximately 100 bytes. "Getting Started with the IBM PC and XT by David Arnold and the Editors of PC World" can fit on this tiny space with room to spare. The fact that we can store information so compactly has two implications. If the information isn't well organized, finding anything can be a nightmare, but if the information is well organized, search time can be almost instantaneous.

At first it may seem that the most efficient way to use your disks is to keep adding files until you fill one disk, then start another, and then another. That method is as efficient as dumping all your paper files—from carbons and contracts to receipts and reports—into one file drawer. You'll need an electronic filing system, and like all organizational schemes, it can be implemented more easily when you are beginning a project rather than after confusion has taken hold.

"A place for everything and everything in its place" is only half the secret of a successful filing system. You also have to know where that place is. Mark Twain's system, "Have a place for everything, and keep it somewhere else," isn't funny to those who use it. Rather than divide and conquer, the tasks are divide and catalog.

With paper files, dividing takes the form of file folders and file drawers, while cataloging is accomplished with labels on the folders and the drawers, perhaps aided by a collection of index cards or a notebook.

With an electronic filing system, the key element is the disk. The trick is to file like items with like items so that all files on a given disk have some relation to one another. Although the details of your particular classification scheme will depend upon what you do with your PC, some general principles and techniques can help you develop that system.

Organizing Electronic Files

Electronic files fall into two basic categories: programs and data. It is usually best to keep these two kinds of files on separate disks. Set up a program disk for each type of work, such as word processing, financial calculations, and data base operations. Format the disk using the /S option, and add any additional DOS files you might want, such as DISKCOPY, CHKDSK, and FORMAT. You'll also have your applications program or two or more related programs and utilities on the disk. This setup will give you computing power and convenience but will leave little room to store the work that you create. To have the entire disk available for storage, use disks formatted without the system (without the /S). Some PC users put the operating system on their data disks and on their program disks. This arrangement may provide some extra convenience, but it uses up almost 12 percent of the otherwise available storage space.

The program disk goes in drive A and the data disk in drive B. If you have a one-drive system or a hard disk, you'll have to do things a little differently. (Single-drive systems are discussed later in this chapter, and hard disks are covered in Chapter 9.)

Most kinds of work eventually generate enough files to fill a number of disks. By strictly separating data disks from program disks, you'll keep floppy confusion to a minimum while maximizing the computing power at your fingertips.

At the moment, the disk in my A drive contains a word processing program, a spelling program, and several DOS files for formatting, making backups, and other tasks. There are also some other utility programs on the disk, including one that customizes my keyboard by redefining keys for commonly used commands. Because my PC has a multifunction board with a clock, the disk also includes a program that automatically reads the date and the time into memory when I boot the system.

When I use my PC for word processing, this disk is in drive A, and a data disk is in drive B. For other sorts of tasks, I use a similar division of labor, with one program disk and one or more data disks.

This system combines maximum program usage (on drive A) with maximum data storage (on drive B). By separating files that require frequent backups from those that don't, backup efforts are kept to a minimum. The program disks are created from the DOS disk and the original program disks from the software manufacturers, so if anything happens to a working program disk, it could easily be reconstructed. The data disks, however, contain information that exists nowhere else; therefore having at least two current backup copies of all these disks is essential.

If you have two types of disks and copies of each, you will need a system of disk identification. There are four places where you can catalog electronic files: on the inside of the disk (an electronic directory), on the outside of the disk (a label), on the storage envelope, or in a separate location (such as a notebook).

The PC and the XT automatically provide one kind of file catalog: the DOS directory. But if you use only the directory to keep track of files, you'll spend countless hours doing the "disk search shuffle," inserting disk after disk and typing DIR, looking for a particular file.

The DOS directory, useful as it is, has two shortcomings. You can view only the directory of the disk that is currently in the computer, and the directory provides a limited amount of information about each file: the eight-character file name, the three-character extension, the size of the file, and the date on which the file was created or last modified.

One shortcut in the disk search shuffle is printing the directory of each disk and attaching it to the disk storage envelope. Although you can send material from the PC to a printer in several ways, one especially convenient method is using the <PrtSc> (print screen) key. Provided that your printer is turned on and properly connected, pressing <Shift>-<PrtSc> will direct the computer to print whatever is currently displayed on the screen (the technical term is *screen dump*).

By pressing <Ctrl>-<PrtSc>, you can use the printer almost as a typewriter; anything new that appears on the screen will also be printed on paper. This *echo* function will continue until you press <Ctrl>-<PrtSc> a second time to turn it off. You can use these functions to print a directory, which can then be taped to the outside of the storage envelope. Because standard-sized type will make the directory too large to fit, either use condensed type (if your printer has this feature), or fold the directory and place it inside the envelope. You can print the directories of many disks by typing DIR, waiting while the disk's directory prints, then putting in a different disk and typing DIR again.

You can make the disk directory more useful by using a set of symbols or abbreviations as part of the file names. There are at least three ways to do this. One is using the extension to designate the particular type of file, such as .INV for invoices, .CON for contracts, and .LET for letters. But some programs make automatic backup copies of every file and give them the extension .BAK. If you use such a program and have a file called CLIENT23.LET and another called CLIENT23.INV, the program would create a single backup file called CLIENT23.BAK. Whether this file contains invoices or letters will depend upon which file you worked on last. If the programs you use don't create .BAK files, using the extension as a cataloging device can be a useful tool.

Another approach is making the first character of every file name a symbol that indicates the file type. In *Writing in the Computer Age*, Andrew Fluegelman and Jeremy Joan Hewes suggest beginning invoice file names with $, letters with @, and project notes with &. Beginning file names with these or other special characters, you can develop a code that fits your particular tasks.

A third technique, which can be combined with the previous one, is indicating the date in the filespec. This method is of little value when you look at a DOS directory, since DOS automatically adds the date to each file name, but many applications programs don't display this information as part of their directories. When you are writing with *WordStar* (MicroPro) or *Spellbinder* (Lexisoft), for example, the directory displayed does not include the date; to retrieve it you would have to switch to DOS, type DIR, and after reading the directory return to the word processing program. I put the month in the first space of the extension and the day in the next two. A file created on the fourth of July would have the extension .704. After passing September, I use letters to designate the month: Christmas day would be D25. Knowing the year is usually not a problem, but if I am ever in doubt I can check the DOS listing.

Regardless of how you catalog your disks, be sure to label each one adequately. A box of ten disks usually comes with two or more labels per disk, so use and update the labels freely. As soon as I format a blank disk, I label it with an "F." If the formatting includes the system, I mark the label "F/S." Since my disk envelopes have directories on the outside, I don't try to duplicate this information on the label; I strive for readability. I record only the main purpose of the disk—just enough to enable me to reunite it with the correct envelope. The disk currently in my A drive is labeled "WordStar Work Disk" and "F/S." The B disk's label reads "WordStar Files for Getting Started...; Chapts. 3, 4, 5," with an "F" in the corner. Since I back up the data disk every day, it also contains a string of dates with all but the last one crossed out. When the label is full or nearly unreadable, I peel it off and attach a new one.

Since labels come in a variety of colors, you can easily color code your disks, using one color for master backups, another for working program disks, and a third for data disks. Or use one color for spreadsheet disks (backups, program disks, and data disks), another for word processing, and so forth.

Labels and directory printouts solve the disk search shuffle problem, but they still rely on the file information provided by DOS. If this isn't adequate for your purposes, you can create an annotated directory as a separate file on each disk, with a sentence or two describing each file's contents plus any other information that may be useful. You might want to list the date on which the file was first created and last updated. If more than one person has access to the files, the initials of the person who created or last used each file can be included. If you set up annotated directories, be sure to update them after every work session.

To solve both cataloging problems—accessibility and adequacy of information—you can use the <PrtSc> key to generate hard copies of each annotated directory. Print one directory to a sheet, and store all of them in a notebook next to the computer.

Backing Up Electronic Files
While you are creating or modifying files, your work resides in RAM, or current memory. If the power is interrupted, everything in RAM will disappear. It is essential that you save your work often by transferring the data in RAM to the data disk. Some programs allow you to save data with a single key, while others require a two- or three-key sequence. Whatever the technique, develop a regular system for saving your work. Some people set a timer to remind them every 10 or 20 minutes, some save every time they fill up a screen, and others just save whenever they have made a significant change or addition. Besides saving regularly, get into the habit of saving any time you are interrupted. If the phone rings, someone comes to the door, or you get up to stretch, save your data.

Once your work is stored on a disk, it is relatively secure—but only relatively. A wayward cup of coffee, a magnetized pair of scissors, an incorrect instruction typed into the computer, or even an occasional flaw in the disk can transform days of work into a third-rate Frisbee. This doesn't happen very often, but once is bad enough.

The solution is to develop a system of backups that keeps possible loss within acceptable bounds. One way is to make two copies of each data disk: a working disk and a backup. At the end of each session, or whatever period you decide on, copy all the information from your working disk to your backup disk, then store the two disks in different locations. Although this is probably the most common system, it leaves you open to one danger: while you are making the backup, both copies of your data are in the computer. Conceivably, either a power surge or an operator error could damage the information on both disks. For critical information, a rotating system with two or more backups is preferable.

The two basic tools for creating backups are the DOS commands DISKCOPY and COPY, which you used in Chapters 2 and 3. DISKCOPY duplicates an entire disk and formats the disk at the same time. When you need a backup, DISKCOPY is a single command that works every time and requires no additional information or decisions. But as we will see, it is not the best command to use for all purposes.

Before DISKCOPY puts anything new on a disk, it erases what is already there. While this is one of the most convenient operations in DOS, it is also one of the most dangerous. The very name focuses our attention on the command's copying function and makes us forget that it also erases. COPY can also do away with data if a file already has the same name as your new target file. If you enter **COPY A:MYFILE B:**, for example, and the disk in drive B already has a file named MYFILE, the original MYFILE on drive B will be written over by the new file, with that name being copied from drive A.

COPY works on only formatted disks. If you try to copy a file onto a new disk (not yet formatted), DOS will display the message 'Disk error reading drive n' (*n* represents the letter of the drive containing the unformatted disk). Unlike DISKCOPY, COPY duplicates only those files that you specify, not the entire disk. If you want to back up a single file, use the COPY command.

DOS also offers *global characters* or *wild cards*. Let's say you want to copy three files—SAMSMITH, JANSMITH, and PAT-SMITH—from drive A to drive B. Instead of using the COPY command three separate times, you can enter **COPY A:???SMITH B:** <Enter>, and DOS will copy all three. DOS interprets a question mark the way a card player interprets a joker—as a wild card that can be substituted for any other character. Similarly, a command using the file-spec HENRY.??? will be applied to HENRY.COM, HENRY.BAT, HENRY.TXT, or whatever HENRYs you might happen to have.

Question marks provide character-by-character substitution, but what if the number of characters varies? If you want to copy TOM, DICK, and HARRY, the question mark won't work. DOS recognizes a second global character: the asterisk. The question mark tells DOS, "replace me with anything you can find," and the asterisk says, "replace me and all the characters to my right with anything you can find." Typing **COPY A:* B:** <Enter> will cause TOM,

DICK, HARRY, and any other files without extensions to be copied from drive A to drive B. Because the asterisk designates all characters on one side of the period, to duplicate everything on a disk, you would type **COPY A:*.* B:**<Enter>.

Similarly, typing **ERASE *.BAS** <Enter> will erase all the BASIC programs on the default drive, while typing the most dangerous DOS command of all, **ERASE *.*** <Enter>, will wipe the disk clean (but only after you reply affirmatively to the query 'Are you sure (Y/N)?_'. Actually, it won't always erase everything. Remember those hidden files IBMBIOS.COM and IBMDOS.COM? They are protected and can be written over only by FORMAT or DISKCOPY.

There are a few more differences between COPY and DISK-COPY that are worth remembering. But first we need to examine the way in which DOS places files on a disk. Let's say you have three files on the disk: TOM, DICK, and HARRY. You no longer need DICK, which occupies 3072 bytes, so you erase it. Later you create a 4096-byte file named ROGER. DOS will start storing ROGER in the first available sectors, which may be the 3K space left by the demise of DICK. When it fills up that area, it will skip over the occupied sectors and store the final 1K of ROGER after the end of HARRY. Thus, the ROGER file will be fragmented. DOS can keep track of all this, so you don't have to worry about losing ROGER's hindquarter. But accessing fragmented files is slower than working with contiguous files, because more movement is required of the disk drive. Therefore, if you need to revise a number of files on a disk, bear in mind that fragmentation can cause a significant time lag.

Because DISKCOPY creates an exact duplicate, each file occupies the same tracks and sectors on the new version as it did on the old, leaving fragmented files fragmented. COPY, on the other hand, consolidates files. Once it starts copying ROGER, it will copy all of ROGER into consecutive sectors before starting on HARRY. There will be no fragmented files or gaps on the disk, and access times will be shorter.

But there is a price to pay for this service. If your target disk is already formatted, COPY *.* can take two to three minutes, depending on how much is on the disk, while DISKCOPY gets the job done in 60 seconds flat. If you need to format the disk first, the waiting time is even longer.

While COPY is an internal command, DISKCOPY is external. To take advantage of DISKCOPY's speed, you have to have the file DISKCOPY.COM in one of your drives. COPY resides in memory and is always immediately available. In short, DISKCOPY is simpler and faster, while COPY is safer, more flexible, and eliminates fragmentation.

A Note on Single-Drive Systems

Most of the examples so far have focused on systems having two disk drives. If your system has only one drive, you can do all the same things, but not as easily. To grasp the difference between one- and two-drive systems, imagine a photocopy machine that can reproduce only a half-sheet of paper at a time. You have to insert the original, press a button, and remove the original. Then insert a blank sheet, press a button, and remove the copy. Reinsert the original, press a button, and remove; reinsert the now half-blank sheet, press a button, and remove—and so on. Not the efficiency you've come to expect, but think what an improvement that machine is over not having one at all.

A single-drive computer is much like our mythical half-sheet copy machine. It's a tremendous improvement over not having one, but not the efficient tool it could be. To duplicate a disk, type **DISKCOPY** <Enter>, and the screen will prompt you to 'Insert source diskette in A'. Insert the disk you want copied, press a key, and wait while a portion of the disk is copied into memory. Then you are asked to 'Insert target diskette in A, strike any key when ready'. Then back to the original, then the copy again, and perhaps again, depending upon the amount of memory installed in your PC.

Batch Files

As with any tool or resource, using the computer effectively comes down to having it do what it is good at, so it can free you to do more of what you are good at. The computer is useful for repetitious tasks. By now you have probably had enough experience with DOS to realize that entering DOS commands is exactly the sort of task better left to the computer. Not only is repeatedly entering the same set of DOS commands an inefficient use of your abilities, it is also an invitation to make errors.

How can we get DOS to issue DOS commands? The trick is the batch file. DOS commands are usually entered one at a time from the keyboard. If you have several, the usual procedure is issuing one command, waiting for the result, then issuing the next, and so on. If you have to do this frequently, you'll be wasting time and effort as well as opening the way for mistakes. But batch files can combine commands for you. A *batch file* is simply a series of commands that DOS accepts all at once and then executes sequentially as though you had entered the commands yourself.

Let's try it. Put your working DOS disk (with a write-protect sticker on it) in drive A and a blank disk in drive B. Use the DISK-COPY command to make a backup copy (DISKCOPY A: B:), and then put away the original disk, which is in drive A. Now if you make any mistakes or don't like what you create on the new disk, you can start over without fear of wiping out your original disk.

Up to now you have used the COPY command to copy files from one disk to another. COPY A:FILE1 B:FILE2 looks for a file named FILE1 on the disk in drive A, copies it onto the disk in drive B, and names the copy FILE2. Batch files are also created with the COPY command, but instead of copying from a disk we will copy from the "console," an archaic name for the keyboard and the screen. With your new working disk in drive A, type

COPY CON BATCHDEM.BAT <Enter>.

As usual, you are telling DOS to copy from the location on the left to the location on the right. But instead of the source's being something already on a disk file, it is something you will create on the console (COPY CON refers to console). The command also tells DOS to name this yet-to-be-created file BATCHDEM.BAT. BATCHDEM, like all file names, is a string of one to eight characters that reminds us of the file's contents—in this case, that it's a demonstration batch file. All batch files must be given the extension .BAT.

After you enter a line beginning with COPY CON, DOS does not return another A prompt, because it can't execute the command until you enter the contents of the file. Don't disappoint it; enter two more lines:

DIR A:/W <Enter>

DIR B:/W <Enter>

To complete the batch file press <**F6**> <**Enter**>. The characters ^Z will appear on the screen, drive A will operate for a few seconds as DOS copies your series of commands from the console to the disk, and the A prompt will reappear, signifying that DOS has completed your last command and is waiting for another. The <F6> key in a batch file is the equivalent of <Ctrl>-Z (also written ^Z), which is an "end of file marker." It tells DOS that you have reached the end of the file that you wanted to copy from the console. DOS then stores that file on a disk and returns to its normal mode of operation.

Now run your batch file by typing **BATCHDEM** <**Enter**>. (If a filespec ends in .BAT, .COM, or .EXE, you do not have to type the extension; DOS will automatically look for extensions and knows what to do with them.) Your screen should now display information similar to that shown in Figure 4.1.

When you typed BATCHDEM, DOS searched the disk and found the file. Since it had the extension .BAT, DOS handled the file in a special way: it read the first line, treated it as a command and executed it, and then went on to the next line. When no commands were left, it displayed the A prompt, thus turning control back to

```
A>COPY CON BATCHDEM.BAT
DIR A:/W
DIR B:/W
^Z
        1 file(s) copied

A>BATCHDEM

A>DIR A:/W

Volume in drive A has no label
Directory of A:

A>DIR B:/W

Volume in drive B has no label
Directory of B:

A> _
```

Figure 4.1 *An example of creating and using a batch file. The final line of the batch file is always displayed as ^Z even though it can be entered with function key <F6>.*

you. This batch file consisted of two commands, each requesting a directory, so DOS displayed two directories. If you would like to see those two directories again, instead of specifying one command, waiting, and then entering the second, just type **BATCHDEM** <Enter>, and DOS will handle it for you.

A batch file can contain any number of regular DOS commands and also special commands that are unique to batch files. You can begin a line with REM, add any remark you wish, and when you run the batch file, that line will appear on the screen. You can type PAUSE, and when the batch file reaches it, DOS will do exactly that—pause—and display the line 'Strike a key when ready…'.

The basic idea of batch files is to let the computer do a series of tasks for you so that you won't have to interact with the computer separately for each command. But sometimes neither the interactive nor the batch mode is quite what you want. Perhaps you end almost every session by copying two files but their names always differ. Perhaps they are critical files, so you also want to verify the contents of the original and the backup after each copy, then examine the directories of both disks. You can create a batch file to do all of this by using *replaceable parameters.* Type

    COPY CON COPY2&CK.BAT <Enter>
    COPY A:%1 B:/V <Enter>

```
COPY A:%2 B:/V <Enter>
DIR A:/P <Enter>
DIR B:/P <Enter>
<F6> <Enter>
```

Since A is your default drive, you could leave off the A's. On the other hand, they don't hurt, so until you are comfortable with DOS notation it's wise to include them. The symbols %1 and %2 are replaceable parameters. When you run the batch file, you can include the names of the files you want to copy as part of your command, and DOS will use those files in place of %1 and %2. If you are working with two contracts labeled CLIENT-A.CON and CLIENT-B.CON, you can type **COPY2&CK CLIENT-A.CON CLIENT-B.CON** **<Enter>**, and DOS will insert those names in the COPY command.

Reorganizing Electronic Files

Using paper files, you often end up looking for something under one classification when it is actually stored under another. The invoices for Wobbly Widgets, Ltd., are stored in the Wobbly Widgets folder. If you wanted to review the invoices that went out in July, you'd go to the Wobbly Widgets folder, flip through scores of letters, purchase orders, and invoices, and pull out the invoices from July, making sure to mark their location in the file. Then you'd do the same with the Dubious Doorknob folder and all the other accounts.

Electronic files make the job easier. You can use a separate disk for each type of customer. Whenever you create an invoice, you can identify it as such in the filespec, perhaps by beginning each invoice's file name with a dollar sign. Load DOS into memory, then put an empty but formatted disk in drive B, and the first of your customer data disks in drive A. While logged onto A (with A as your default drive), type **COPY $*.* B:** <**Enter**>. All the invoices, and only the invoices, will be copied to drive B. Replace the disk in drive A with your next customer disk, and repeat the process. You don't have to type out the command again. DOS always saves the last command in memory; you can retrieve it by pressing <F3>. Now press <Enter>, and the invoices on this disk will also be copied onto the disk in drive B.

If you follow this procedure for each customer disk, you will have all your invoices in one place. How do you separate the July invoices? If you use the extension to indicate the date, it will be easy. Just copy the invoices using question marks or asterisks in the extension—for example, **COPY *.7*** if you use 7 to indicate July.

Because reorganizing electronic files is so easy, it's a good idea to make periodic reorganizations part of your routine. At the end of a given period, perhaps weekly or even quarterly, make it a practice to reorganize your files. This corresponds to the paper filing procedure of pulling files and documents from the top file drawer or front cabinet, regrouping them, and storing them in the bottom drawer or one of the back file cabinets.

For example, you could use COPY and ERASE to move all letters written in the last quarter from the various client disks where they originated to a single disk entitled 2NDQTR84.LTR. This would clear noncurrent files off the current disk while maintaining accessibility. You might want to add a short file to each client disk that lists the letters that have been removed: addressee, date, subject, and current location of the file.

The previous example assumes that your files were originally organized by person or organization. If your files are organized by type (letters, memos, expenses, articles, and so on), it might make sense to reorganize periodically by person or organization.

Try the various methods, experiment, and work out your own approach. Because a system used only sporadically is worse than none at all, be sure to develop a system that you can stick to.

CHAPTER FIVE

An Introduction to Software

You've probably heard of second-generation hardware and software, but have you heard of third-generation computer users? Many of the first microcomputer users were hobbyists. These people bought their computers primarily because they wanted to learn everything they could about this technology. The next people to buy computers were also hobbyists, but their interests were primarily in software rather than hardware. Some enjoyed programming; others preferred games. Many software hobbyists used their computers for challenging but nonessential applications such as turning their lights on and off or cross-indexing their Christmas card list.

Then spreadsheets and word processing programs came along, and with them a third generation of computer users. These people bought computers—not to learn about the hardware or have fun with the software, but to use them as productivity tools. They entered the local computer shop thinking a cursor was a dissatisfied user and a floppy some kind of rabbit. This led to a demand for "user-friendly" software—programs that enabled professionals to use computers without having to become programmers. The idea was to make the program fit the user, not the other way around.

Menus vs. Commands

One of the primary ways to make programs easier to use is to provide a list of operations (a menu). In Chapter 2 you used a menu-driven utility, the IBM Diagnostics program. At each step the program displayed a series of alternatives; you simply had to enter the number of the alternative you wanted or type Y or N in response to a question.

Since menu-driven programs are so simple, why does anyone produce or buy anything else? We can answer that by looking at the program you used next, the command-driven disk operating system, or DOS. Whereas the Diagnostics program's initial display was a

Figure 5.1 *A hypothetical menu for using the COPY command.*

```
To copy a file, select an option:
1 - Copy from drive A to drive B
2 - Copy from drive B to drive A
3 - Copy from A to A (file names or extensions must differ)
4 - Copy from B to B (file names or extensions must differ)
5 - Return to previous menu
Enter the action desired (1–5): _
Enter name of old file: _ _ _ _ _ _ _ _ . _ _ _
Enter name of new file: _ _ _ _ _ _ _ _ . _ _ _
After copying, do you want the copy verified (Y/N)? _
Are all above entries correct (Y/N)? _
```

reasonably clear set of choices, the initial DOS display is a cryptic A prompt.

IBM could have given us a menu-driven DOS, but would it really be an improvement? Perhaps, but the menu would need three dozen alternatives. The selections wouldn't all fit on the screen at once and would have to be divided into groups: commands to get information (DIR, CHKDSK), commands to move or change files (COPY, RENAME, ERASE), advanced commands, miscellaneous commands, and more. We would first need a master menu to choose among the groups, then several other menus for the specific commands within each group. Let's say you selected the move or change files option. The second-level menu would have several alternatives, including copying a file. That would lead to a third-level menu, perhaps like the one in Figure 5.1. Such a menu would be useful but would probably have too much information to plow through. Adding the global character options, ? and *, would further complicate the process. You would probably find it quicker and easier to type **COPY FILENAME.EXT B:**.

Still, a menu-driven program is easier to learn, and you won't forget how to operate it if you don't use the program for a while. For programs that present a limited range of alternative actions, the menu-driven format has almost no drawbacks. Yet any program feature involves a trade-off. Menus require disk and RAM space, and they reduce speed. Often the cost is worth it, but in some instances it isn't.

Function Keys vs. Control Sequences

A second technique in making software easy to learn is extensive use of programmed function keys. For example, one common word processing program uses the command <Ctrl>-R to move to the previous page. Moving to the beginning of the file in this program requires holding down the <Ctrl> key and pressing Q, then R. But the PC's special keys are used for alternative versions of certain commands in this program: pressing <PgUp> moves to the previous page, while pressing <F10> moves to the end of the file.

Function keys, like menus, involve a trade-off. They reduce learning time, but if you'll be using the program regularly, the added time it takes to become proficient on command-driven or control-key sequence programs is likely to be repaid in increased efficiency.

Many programs now offer the best of both worlds: friendliness for the new or occasional user and efficiency for the regular user. The word processor just described is one example; some others are described in the next chapter.

Sampling Software

A personal computer is nothing but a box in which to run software; without a program, it just sits there. When IBM introduced the PC in August 1981, only nine applications programs were introduced with it: a spreadsheet, two accounting systems, three educational programs, one communications program, one game, and a word processor. Within two years this number had grown to more than 2000, and today it is well beyond that. Let's examine two programs and then consider how to go about selecting software. Chapter 6 examines some of the nooks and crannies of the software world, introducing the range of applications that the PC can handle.

Let's look first at *Typing Tutor*, an educational program distributed by IBM. Although you don't need the program to follow along, you may get more out of this discussion if you do have it. Almost every PC dealer carries *Typing Tutor*, and at $25 it's a real bargain. Since the program is easy, fun, and practical, it is an excellent introduction to the computer for family, friends, and computer-phobic co-workers.

Before you use *Typing Tutor*, take these two preliminary steps. First make a backup copy. Put your working DOS disk in drive A and type **DISKCOPY A: B:**. In response to the screen prompts, remove the DOS disk, put the original *Typing Tutor* disk in drive A, and a blank, unformatted disk in drive B. Press any key. When the backup process has been completed, the screen will prompt you to return the DOS disk to drive A. (If you have an XT, you can copy the program onto the hard disk, then copy it to another floppy disk for backup.) Put the original *Typing Tutor* disk away for safekeeping.

Most applications programs do not include DOS, and *Typing Tutor* is no exception. So the next step is to add the DOS system files to the *Typing Tutor* program disk. Remember that the main parts of DOS are contained in COMMAND.COM plus the two hidden files. Because the hidden files are protected from the COPY command, there are only two ways to transfer them. The first is by using the command FORMAT/S when you prepare a new disk. You could do that and then use COPY *.* to transfer all the *Typing Tutor* files to the newly formatted system disk. But DOS provides a special command, SYS, that allows you to transfer the system to a program disk. As long as the original is prepared in a manner that leaves room for the DOS files (IBMBIO.COM and IBMDOS.COM have to come at the beginning of the disk), the SYS command will place these files where they belong.

Actually, *Typing Tutor* makes this process still easier by providing a batch file that enters the commands for you. Just type **setup2** (**setup1** for a single-drive system), and follow the directions on the screen. To see what the batch file looks like, type **TYPE setup2.bat** <**Enter**>. While you're at it, you might want to examine one more batch file, AUTOEXEC.BAT, the one that starts *Typing Tutor*. If you don't understand some of the batch commands, refer to Chapters 4 and 10 and to your DOS manual. These two steps, making a backup and transferring DOS, are a bit of a nuisance, but you have to do them only once for each new program.

Now put your *Typing Tutor* program disk in drive A and reboot (<Ctrl>-<Alt>-<Del>). If you watch closely, you'll see the A prompt followed by 'basic tt'. Then that disappears, and the program starts running. If earlier you asked DOS to **TYPE AUTOEXEC.BAT**, what you saw was just that file's one line: 'basic tt'. 'Basic' tells DOS to load BASIC.COM into RAM, and 'tt' tells it to load and run tt.bas, the *Typing Tutor* program, which is written in BASIC.

Typing Tutor is a good example of a menu-driven program. After an initial message showing the IBM logo and a copyright notice, the screen asks if you are a new user. If you answer "yes," the program prompts you to enter your name, then choose whether you want to learn '1. Letters', '2. Numbers', or '3. Symbols'. Throughout the program, you make choices by entering the appropriate number.

The program will store your name on the disk, so next time you use it, it will start by offering a choice between '1. New User' and '2. your name'. For some reason, even if you enter your name in capital letters, the program stores it in lowercase letters. Eventually, the opening menu might look like Figure 5.2.

Notice that the prompt specifies that the user select a number between 1 and 7. Since only '1. New User' is listed the first time the program is run, the last line reads 'Select (1):_'. When evaluating any menu-driven program, make sure that each menu provides adequate guidance and that the program has thorough *error handling*—that errors won't cause the program to *crash* (end and return you to DOS) or make the keyboard so unresponsive (often called *locked up*) that you have to reboot. This program handles errors well: if instead of giving *Typing Tutor* an appropriate number you entered something else (8, 1776, A, or your name), it would ignore the input. Some programs go a step further, handling improper responses by displaying a message that explains why your input was unacceptable.

After the user number is selected, *Typing Tutor* replaces the opening menu with one asking whether you want typing lessons, a practice paragraph, or a typing test. If you enter 1 for typing lessons, the information shown in Figure 5.3 will appear.

Typing Tutor presents you with three columns on its lesson screen. The center column, LESSON KEYS, contains the letters you are to practice—in a list near the top of the screen and in two other sequences near the bottom. The right column, labeled SLOW, contains all the keyboard characters except those in the center column. The left column, FAST, is empty until you develop proficiency with some of the lesson keys.

Type **sadf dsfa** <**Enter**>. *Typing Tutor* will tell you the number of errors, mark each one, report your speed in words per minute, and present a new set of letters for you to type. When you have become proficient at typing any character, it is transferred to the FAST column, and a new character is moved from SLOW to LESSON KEYS.

After you have completed ten lessons, another menu will appear with six choices:

> 1. Continue lesson
> 2. Build more speed
> 3. Learn more keys
> 4. Practice paragraph
> 5. Typing test
> 6. Progress report
> Select (1-6)_

'Build more speed' raises the threshold for transferring a key from slow to fast; 'Learn more keys' lowers it. You can learn the entire

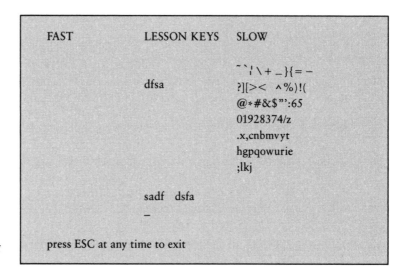

Figure 5.2 *A sample opening menu for the* Typing Tutor *program.*

1. New User
2. your name
3. your name, jr.
4. jim
5. sarah
6. thomas a. watson
7. e. e. cummings
Select (1–7): _

Figure 5.3 *A sample typing lesson with* Typing Tutor.

FAST	LESSON KEYS	SLOW

dfsa

~ ` ¦ \ + _ }{ = –
?][>< ^%)!(
@*#&$”:65
01928374/z
.x,cnbmvyt
hgpqowurie
;lkj

sadf   dsfa

_

press ESC at any time to exit

keyboard first, typing at a slow or moderate pace, and then go through the lessons again to increase your speed.

The practice paragraph consists of characters, words, and phrases from your current FAST and LESSON KEYS columns. Each time you request a practice paragraph, *Typing Tutor* analyzes your current typing level and constructs a custom paragraph. It accomplishes this feat in about seven seconds. Quite an improvement over typing class back in high school.

If you select '6. Progress report', the program presents a list of the keys you have learned, average speed, percent accuracy, corrected speed, and best speed. If at any time you had taken the typing test, it would also show your speed, accuracy, and corrected speed on the test.

If you exercise the 'Esc' option during a lesson, *Typing Tutor* goes directly to the six-choice menu. Press <Esc> again, and you get three choices:

65   *An Introduction to Software*

1. Return to lesson
2. Record progress
3. Quit

Choice number 1 is an example of error handling: it lets you correct your mistake if you press <Esc> accidentally. Number 3 ends the program. Number 2 also ends the program, but first it records the information from your progress report onto the disk. The next time you run *Typing Tutor* it will start exactly where you left off, rather than making you repeat material you learned during the previous lesson.

This discussion should give you a good overview of *Typing Tutor*. Now let's look at a program at the other end of the spectrum in cost, power, flexibility, and difficulty. The program is *dBASE II* (Ashton-Tate), a best-selling data base management program.

Like *Typing Tutor, dBASE II* requires that you transfer the system to it. As with any program, making a backup copy first, while not required, is strongly recommended. Many people routinely make two backups of all new program disks. The original disk should be stored in a separate location; unless a problem arises, it need not be used again. The first backup becomes the master and is used only to make other backups. The second backup becomes the working disk.

Boot your *dBASE II* program disk by turning on the computer or giving the reboot command (<Ctrl>-<Alt>-<Del>). All you get are the usual date and time queries followed by the A prompt—no logo, no menu, no guidance of any sort. Just to get the program started you have to know the right command. But this one is easy: **DBASE** <Enter>. The disk will whirl for a bit, and then you'll get one line with '* * *DBASE II', a version number, and a release date, and a second line with only a period. This period is the *dBASE* prompt. Just as the A prompt indicates that DOS is present, the period means that *dBASE II* is ready for your command.

To use DOS you had to know a series of commands and the rules for stringing together the commands, drive designators, and file names. The same is true for using *dBASE II*. This program's primary operations are storing and manipulating information, which it does by establishing data bases—collections of information in formats designated by the program. To create a data base, type **CREATE**, and the program will prompt you for the necessary information. You'll need to know the proper syntax, but you needn't memorize all the details. *dBASE II* uses commands such as APPEND and INSERT to add information to a data base, and EDIT, CHANGE, MODIFY STRUCTURE, and REPLACE to change the structure or contents of a data base. Once the data base is set up, commands such as USE, DISPLAY, and FIND allow you to locate and view information, while another series of commands provides printed reports.

dBASE II allows you to store a number of files and recombine them at will. Let's say you own a computer store, and Harry Hacker, one of your regular customers, calls the order department. If you were using *dBASE II* to manage your store's records, you could key in Harry's name, and the computer would display his address, account status, and any other information you specified when you used the CREATE command. You could also have developed a specialized order form to enable you to take customers' orders over the phone. Using *dBASE II,* you could also calculate prices, sales tax, and shipping charges, and print an address form.

The author of *dBASE II* had no way of knowing if you would want to use the program to enter, calculate, and record sales, and prepare invoices and shipping information. What he did, therefore, was leave you as many options as possible, which means many commands. All of *Typing Tutor*'s options could be presented in a half-dozen simple menus. This could be done with *dBASE II* only if its options were as limited as *Typing Tutor*'s.

The sales and order system just described might take an experienced *dBASE II* user many hours to develop. Once such a system has been developed, however, it can be stored in an easy-to-use format. And while the entire *dBASE II* program cannot be menu-driven, limited applications, such as this one, can.

Between *Typing Tutor* and *dBASE II* fall literally thousands of other programs, ranging from fixed to flexible, from single-purpose to multifaceted. Some provide all the training you'll need right on the screen. With others you have to study thick manuals before you can use them, and learning them fully requires experience, classes, or both. With so many choices, it is easy to make the wrong one.

Choosing Software
The following considerations should help you make informed, judicious software choices:

Analyze your needs. Don't buy a truck if a station wagon will do, but don't buy a station wagon to haul aircraft engines. While computer programs have a lot of flexibility, each one has its strong and weak points and is best for specific tasks.

Analyze your future needs. Computer needs tend to grow to fill and exceed available hardware and software capacity. If you have 2300 customers today, a program that can handle 4000 is probably too small.

Analyze the program's features. What does it do and what doesn't it do? Which of these things do you need, which would be nice, and which would merely get in the way?

Analyze the program's ease of use. Does it require special installation or customizing for your situation, or can you pop a disk in the computer and start using it right away? How difficult is it to learn? Once you learn it, how difficult is it to use?

Analyze your equipment in relation to the program. Will the program work properly on your PC as it is presently configured, or will you have to buy more memory, a color graphics board, or a coprocessor chip? If you have an XT or an external hard disk, can the program be copied, or will you always have to run it on the original floppy disk?

Analyze your particular environment. Will one person or many people use the program? If your employees will use the software, consider your rate of turnover. Will audit trails or password protection be necessary?

Analyze software reviews. Reviewers are usually reasonably objective and experienced, but their needs and preferences may not be the same as yours. Use caution with multipage tables comparing features of competing software. Two word processors may each "move columns," but one may do it with a couple of keystrokes while the other requires a dozen or more.

Analyze the documentation. Good documentation orients, trains, and supports. It should help you to understand the program, not just to use it by rote. Even documentation that passes other tests often fails this one. Look for a clear overview at the beginning and perhaps a map of the program, showing how its various modes, functions, and commands are connected. The program should include a tutorial that covers the sorts of tasks for which you will use the program. Finally, it should provide complete and efficient assistance whenever you have a question. This means a good table of contents and an even better index.

Try it. Whatever the program, feed it enough data to test it adequately, preferably using some of your own work. With a word processing program you can type a short paragraph, copy it, then copy the copy. Repeat this a few times, and you will soon have a large enough block of text to simulate any document you might create. Use similar techniques with other kinds of programs.

Find out about available support. Support is a computer buzzword that can have two meanings, one before you buy and another after. The salesperson's "Don't worry, we'll train you and your staff" may turn out to be a 30-minute demonstration in the showroom. Who will do the training? How well do they know the program? How well can they teach? Is the dealer able and willing to handle questions as they arise? For how long? If the dealer isn't, is the manufacturer? If there is an 800 number hot line, try it. Can you get through? Are they helpful when you reach them?

Find out about support not only for the program in its present form but also for updates. If bugs are found or new enhancements added, what will the new version cost you? Some vendors will guarantee a free update if a revision comes out "soon" after purchase. On the other hand, one large software manufacturer, known for issuing frequent revisions of a $495 program, charges as much as $85 for each update.

Whether you need to improve your typing or your customer records, with a little time and effort you should be able to narrow the choice to two or three programs. After that, look at price, the color of the package, or just flip a coin. Remember, most people think the programs they use are wonderful. You probably will too.

CHAPTER SIX

A Guided Tour of Software

Most people decide to start using a computer because they have a particular application in mind, one that the computer can do faster, better, more easily, more inexpensively, or some combination thereof. But although people usually buy computers for one task, once they start using these machines, they almost always find other uses.

You can hasten full utilization of your computer by familiarizing yourself with not only programs you know you can use but also those you may want to use later. Along with computer literate, computer comfortable, and computer competent, aim to become computer familiar. Toward this end, this chapter presents a guided tour of the kinds of software available for the PC. (See the Appendix for a complete list of the software mentioned in this text, including access information.)

The most common uses of personal computers are to manipulate words, numbers, or other information (collectively called *applications programs*) and to provide education and entertainment. But programs are available for a wide range of other purposes.

Words
Word processing is the closest thing to a universal computer application. Not everyone analyzes numbers or deals with records complex

enough to justify a data base management system. We certainly don't all use modems or play *Pac-Man,* but we all write, and anyone who writes even a little can benefit from a word processor.

The problem with writing is that the words often look different on the page than in your imagination. With a word processor everything you write is tentative. Your words await your approval; if you don't like what you see, revision is easy. When you are satisfied, you can save the work on a disk and print it on paper.

Not only is editing easier with a word processor, but simply getting your words down is easier. After a few days with a word processor, most people find that writer's block, which afflicts everyone to some degree, starts to fade. Maybe it's because we know that making changes is so easy, or because the torture instruments of our early education—paper and pen—are nowhere to be seen. Or maybe it's the televisionlike attraction of the monitor. Whatever the reason, almost everyone who tries it finds writing easier on a computer.

Finally, the finished product is better. How many times have you spotted a typo after finishing a letter and decided not to take the trouble to retype it? Or have you been bothered by the way you phrased something, yet let it go? With a word processor you can revise and reprint and still finish on schedule.

Word processors allow you to take a word, a sentence, or a block of text and move it elsewhere in your text. One of life's little annoyances—keeping track of when to press the carriage return—becomes a thing of the past. The word processing program keeps track of where you are and automatically moves to the next line when the cursor reaches the right margin.

Perhaps the most amazing thing about word processors is their *global search and replace* capability. In writing an article about South Dakota, I typed SD each time I needed to mention the state. When I finished, I directed the computer to replace every SD with South Dakota. If you discover, for example, that in your report on packaging alternatives you neglected to capitalize Styrofoam, the computer can do it for you. To locate a particular point in something you wrote, you no longer have to scan every page; just use the search function.

Which word processor should you buy? That's like asking which highway vehicle to buy. Do you plan to haul preschoolers or prestressed concrete, to drive 6 or 600 miles a day?

A word processor, like many other types of programs, involves trade-offs; maximum power and ease of use are difficult to find in the same program. If you want all the bells and whistles, learning how to use them will take time. Someone who writes legal briefs, endless reports, or books will want a full-featured word processor.

But for an occasional memo or letter, a full-featured program may prove cumbersome and if not used regularly might send you back to that original word processor, the pencil.

While word processors are the primary programs for manipulating words, they are not the only ones. Others include spelling checkers, electronic thesauruses, and even programs that catch grammar errors and sexist terminology. Still other programs handle footnoting and indexing.

These programs are all used for tasks that follow the main writing task. Other programs to use as you begin the writing process include those programs designed for keeping notes. You use them to record notes and then sort and retrieve information. Other programs help organize your thoughts. *The PromptDoc Document Management System* (PromptDoc) asks you questions to help move what is inside your head onto paper. *ThinkTank* (Living Videotext) helps structure your ideas in outline form; you restructure the outline and build paragraphs from the outline headings.

Numbers

While word processing may be the universal computer application, the bottom line in business is money, and money means numbers. In the software world, numbers mean spreadsheets, accounting, and statistics, in that order.

Spreadsheets On one level a spreadsheet is simply a scratch pad. I recall sitting in high school pretending to take notes when I was filling in and analyzing a spreadsheet:

Money available:		Cost of ham radio equipment:	
Amount in bank	42	Second-hand receiver	23
Cash on hand	6	Heathkit transmitter	50
Sell catcher's mitt	8	Key and headphones	12
Sell electric train	20	Parts for antenna	12
Borrow from parents (?)	10		
Gift from Grandma (?)	5		
Total available	91	Total needed	98

Difference (available - needed) = -7

Hmmm, $7 short. If I had sold my skates for $15, I could have kept the mitt. But what if I couldn't have talked Grandma out of $5? And so on, until either the eraser wore out, the paper wore through, or the teacher caught on.

A spreadsheet is a grid, a series of rows and columns similar to a ledger sheet, on which you enter and analyze a collection of figures. Each row-and-column intersection is called a *cell*; you put data in some cells, then arithmetic computations generate new numbers that the program puts in other cells, such as the $7 difference in the simple example above.

If the spreadsheet is on paper, each "what if" requires that you erase one number, enter its replacement, and redo any calculations based on that number. If the spreadsheet is electronic, you just enter the new figure, and the recalculation is done for you. Spreadsheets are ideal for analyzing and forecasting budgets, costs, cash flow, sales, profits and losses, investments, taxes, and almost any task that involves numbers. More importantly, the spreadsheet provides ease and accuracy. You can devise a formula, name the cells to which it applies, and the program will do the calculations.

As with any type of applications program, spreadsheets vary in cost, ease of use, and features (many lack a sorting function, for instance). Spreadsheets also vary in speed of operation. Speed is not too important for programs that process words, but it can be critical for programs that process numbers.

Accounting packages A spreadsheet program can handle many accounting tasks. The advantage of an accounting package is that since it is specifically designed for the application at hand, it is easier to use, faster, and more accurate. Screens are set up for data entry, and extensive error checking is incorporated.

The primary accounting functions are general ledger, accounts payable, accounts receivable, inventory control, and payroll. In many instances, you buy an accounting "package" rather than a single program; the package consists of one program for each of the five functions. If your accounting needs are not too complex, you may be able to use just one or two of the programs, also called *modules*.

Another advantage of an accounting package is that it integrates the various functions. When an order comes in, instead of requiring separate entries in both inventory and accounts payable, the software takes a single entry and automatically posts it wherever relevant. This process prevents errors in addition to saving time and effort.

Since accounting is such an extensive and complex task, accounting packages cost considerably more than other types of programs. Unlike most other programs, the cost savings they offer is not immediate. When people buy word processors, they abandon their typewriters except for filling out one-of-a-kind forms and labels. You certainly wouldn't write the same letter or report twice, once on each machine. But when you switch from manual to automated accounting, that is exactly what you do. Accounting errors are less obvious but more critical. The recommended procedure is to run both systems through two or more accounting periods, checking for discrepancies. Only after the new system has proven error-free should you discontinue the manual system. Consequently, an accounting program will give you neither improved efficiency nor reduced costs for at least six months. But it should more than pay back the cost during the ensuing six months.

Statistical analysis   Clichés such as, "There are lies, damn lies, and statistics," have given this science a bad name. Perhaps a more accurate cliché is, "Statistics don't lie, but liars use statistics." Statistics are merely numbers that summarize other numbers; their job is to simplify. The difficulty with this science is that without a computer the journey from the complex (the original mass of numerical data) to the simple (summarizing numbers) requires that you pass through the still more complex (statistical computations and tables). The computer turns this trip into a simple commute.

There are two kinds of statistics: *descriptive* and *inferential*. The sole job of descriptive statistics is to simplify the presentation of large amounts of data. The best-known example is the mean, or average. Instead of having to examine 700 transactions to get an idea of how much each customer spent in your store last week, a human or electronic assistant totals all the sales, divides by 700, and tells you the average. Statistical programs can also summarize variability. Was the average $15.83 because everyone spent between $15 and $17, or did sales vary from one dollar to hundreds? They can figure percentages, make comparisons, and compute correlations. In short, descriptive statistics do everything their name implies.

The same is true of inferential statistics. While they also describe numerical data, there is a difference. Often your data are samples from a larger population. Perhaps quality control tests one product from each batch, or marketing interviews a fraction of your customers or potential customers. How safe are you in drawing conclusions about the population from the sample? Inferential statistics can give you the answer. And your PC, equipped with a statistical analysis program, can give you the inferential statistics.

Whereas word processors and spreadsheets are general-purpose programs, statistical programs have to be selected with a clear idea of the intended application. Each provides certain statistical measures but not others, and each is intended for specific types of data. Some programs not only analyze the data but also help collect information. *Survtab* (Statistical Computing Consultants), for example, first guides you in constructing a questionnaire, then organizes and summarizes the results.

Personal finance　The types of software discussed so far are programs that manage numbers on the job. While the same programs can handle numbers at home, using a $2000 accounting package to balance your checkbook is both extravagant and ineffective. For a fraction of the price, other programs can do the job better. Standard spreadsheets can be both inexpensive and flexible. For specialized tasks such as income tax or estate planning, specialized programs are very useful. Some tasks can go either way: a general spreadsheet can do an excellent job of charting your investment portfolio, but a single-purpose investment program is easier to use and might offer more specific information.

There is one in-between route: *templates* for use with spreadsheet programs. These are specially developed formats that contain most of the formulas and components for such tasks as checkbook balancing, tax records, and stock market averages. You use a template in conjunction with the spreadsheet program; when you add the data from your pertinent activities, the template and program automatically calculate the results. For common spreadsheet applications, templates are available in books, ready for you to key into your computer, and on disks, ready for immediate use.

Information

Word processing programs manipulate words, and spreadsheets or accounting programs manipulate numbers. Filing programs and data base management systems (DBMSs) manipulate pure information—words or numbers. Seventy-five years ago sociologist Max Weber noted that office management was based upon written documents—the files. That is even truer today: in the information age the control of information equals power.

Filing programs　Filing programs handle lists of information, from stamp collections to personnel records. They can search, retrieve, reorganize, and print reports or labels. Most are menu-driven, easy to learn, and easy to use. For home use and some business uses, they are ideal, but filing programs cannot relate one list of information to another or follow complex instructions. They manage files one at a time.

Data base management systems　DBMSs can keep track of several files at once and follow complex instructions. Think of a DBMS program as you would a human information manager. You can tell the manager that you want the serial numbers of all the tangerine-colored disk drives sold last December to used car dealers in Michigan, and even though it means cross-checking several files and making numerous decisions and comparisons, you'll get your list. The human manager could probably complete the task in several days, while the computerized manager could do it in minutes.

Graphics

Many people are confused about the graphics capability of the PC. As you'll recall from our guided tour of the hardware, using the IBM monochrome monitor requires the board called the Monochrome Display and Printer Adapter, while to operate a color monitor you need what IBM calls the Color/Graphics Adapter. If your PC has only an IBM Monochrome Display and Printer Adapter, you cannot generate high-resolution graphics, but your system can display detailed letters and numbers. You also have access to character graphics, which can generate bar charts, boxes, and borders.

For high-resolution graphics, however, you must have either the IBM Color/Graphics Adapter or some other graphics adapter board. But you do not have to have color to have graphics. You can use a single-color monitor that is capable of displaying graphics with the IBM Color/Graphics Adapter. Several other companies also manufacture adapter boards that provide graphics capability on a color or monochrome screen, whether black and white, green, or amber.

You will also need some way to tell the computer what you want to do. You can use BASIC to display graphics, but that would require writing your own program. As with the applications discussed previously, it often makes more sense to buy a commercial program. A number of such graphics programs are on the market. Some are stand-alone programs—you provide the information (designating shapes, lines, etc.), and they provide the picture. Others are add-on programs—they tie into your data base, spreadsheet, or statistics program, obtain the information from it, and generate a visual display such as a graph or pie chart.

Integrated Programs

Imagine using *dBASE II* (Ashton-Tate) to locate some information, transferring that information to *VisiCalc* (VisiCorp) to develop some projections, then moving to *AbStat* (Anderson-Bell) for some statistical analysis. Now you're ready to boot up *WordStar* (MicroPro) and write your report. Finally, one last step: get out *Super Chartman II* (Mosaic Software), and create a few graphs and bar charts to accompany the report.

This may beat the old way, but wouldn't it be nice if you could avoid having to run five programs to accomplish one job? There is a way: integrated programs.

The object of integrated programs is to have them draw upon each other's results without requiring that you manually enter the output from one program as input for another. The lowest level of integration is compatible data files; compatibility eases the problem but doesn't solve it. While standards are still few and far between in the microcomputer field, many programs generate output that can be read by other programs. In the example above, all five programs can, with certain limitations, read output from the others. You still have to deal with five programs, but at least you don't have to enter the data five separate times.

Certain "families" of programs make this file-switching easier and offer similar commands and structure. Among these software families are the Star products from MicroPro (*WordStar, InfoStar,* and others) and the Easy family (*EasyWriter II, EasyFiler,* and others) from Information Unlimited Software.

The next level is the program integrator, also called an *operating environment,* or *shell.* A master program such as *Microsoft Windows* (Microsoft), *DesQ* (Quarterdeck), or *Visi On* (VisiCorp) ties several other programs together, so that you can move among them as easily as you move from inserting a sentence to formatting a page in your word processor.

Finally, there is the fully integrated program, one that can accomplish many tasks. For example, *1-2-3* (Lotus Development Corporation) is a spreadsheet, a data base manager, and a graphics program.

Naturally, there are trade-offs. The convenience of integration can be expensive and requires additional memory. And integration may sacrifice some power. Although *1-2-3* is a powerful program, some programs have more features and flexibility than its individual components. But integrated programs are the direction of the future. Eventually, we will not think in terms of word processing, spreadsheets, or data base management systems, but of the task at hand.

Communications

Just as integrated programs enable you to transfer data within a computer, communications programs allow you to share data between computers. To make a data transfer you need a communications program, a telephone, and a modem (which converts the computer's digital signals into analog pulses that the phone lines can handle, then converts them back at the other end). We'll look at modems in Chapter 8.

Some modems come with a communications program. You can also buy such a program separately for prices ranging from $35 to $200. This is one area in which more expensive does not necessarily mean better. One of the least expensive communications programs, *PC-Talk III* (The Headlands Press) is one of the best on the market.

Education

Most people think of educational programs in connection with elementary and secondary school curricula, but computer-assisted instruction (CAI) is also applicable to adult education. The *Typing Tutor* program examined in Chapter 5 represents one approach to using the computer as a teaching device—drill and practice. Computers are good at this; they can keep track of levels of achievement and set demands accordingly. They don't get tired, don't lose patience, and don't call it quits at 5 p.m.

Computers are also good at simulation, creating a model of something that can then be manipulated. By varying the model's parameters, the student can simulate its real-world behavior. Computer simulations have been used to study everything from genetics and group behavior to aircraft design. This sort of educational program teaches not only by demonstration but also by the student's active involvement.

Computers can provide useful tutorials with which the student either answers a question or engages in an activity, and the computer's response is keyed to the accuracy of the student's performance.

Unfortunately, many educational programs fall into none of these categories and are what CAI experts call "page turners"— programs that do what could be accomplished at lower cost and with greater portability by an old-fashioned book. Effective educational programs for the computer are highly interactive; the student takes an active role in the learning process. A good educational program can help you learn a wide range of subjects more efficiently than older methods. The problem is that many of the so-called educational programs do not make very good use of the computer's capabilities. This situation should improve dramatically over the next year or so. Meanwhile, be selective.

Entertainment

In general, games fall into three categories. Most popular are the arcade-style games, which emphasize action and graphics. Most of these games require a color graphics board. If you bought a PC to work solely with words and numbers, you probably can't run them. A second category is adventure and fantasy games. Whole families have been known to spend every spare moment for weeks wandering through electronically generated haunted houses, searching for lost treasure. Third are games involving strategy. Many of these are computerized versions of old standbys such as chess and blackjack. Others, such as *Executive Suite* (Armonk Corporation) or *Millionaire* (Blue Chip Software) are new.

Although few, if any, PCs are bought primarily as game machines, adding some games to your software collection is a good idea. They provide not only enjoyment but also a nonthreatening way to introduce novices to the computer.

Utilities

Like utility infielders, utility programs are not limited to one application but can assist in a variety of situations. The applications programs mentioned all do things that you would need to do even if you didn't have a computer; they just do them faster, more accurately, more completely, or less expensively. Utility programs help you indirectly by improving either the computer's operation or your operation of it.

You already have a number of utilities, namely the programs that make up DOS. One essential DOS feature, the disk directory, is not a separate utility but operates like one. As you recall from Chapter 3, it can be displayed in a single column, or if you use the /P or /W options, it can be made to pause after each screen or print across the screen. DOS 2.00 even includes provisions for naming each disk and creating a multilevel, tree-structured directory. (You will learn how to use these features in Chapter 10.) But because an operating system cannot include every possible feature, utility programs have been developed.

One example is disk cataloging programs. IBM sells *Diskette Librarian,* which is sort of a mini data base program. With it you can make a catalog of all your disks' contents, then enter the name of any file, and find out which disk that file is on. *Diskette Manager* (Lassen Software) prints a catalog of all your disks and also prints labels with a title, a list of all the files on the disk, and any comments that you may want to include. These programs may not seem very useful now, but as your disk collection grows, they could help keep things under control.

If your PC has a large amount of memory, you can purchase programs that help partition it. Let's say you have 256K on your system board and another 256K on a plug-in memory board. You can tell the PC to treat 360K of RAM as an additional disk drive (called a *disk emulator*), 128K as normal memory, and whatever is left as a print spooler. The disk emulator acts as a regular drive but operates 10 to 30 times faster. If you regularly use a program that pauses to get information from the disk, you'll find this very helpful, because all of the subsidiary information normally stored on disk can be loaded into the disk emulator along with the main program file.

Another place you may find yourself cooling your heels is while printing. A *print spooler* establishes part of RAM as a *buffer*, or storage area. The file you want to print is transferred to this buffer and from there is fed to the printer. Once the file is in the buffer, the computer is free to be used for other tasks. (DOS 2.00 includes a spooler.)

One of the best things about disk emulators and spoolers is their price. Most add-on memory boards include these utilities at no additional cost.

These examples of utilities just scratch the surface. Other utilities allow you to redefine your keyboard, enter and change messages and other features in commercial applications programs, view the sectors of your disks to see how space is allocated, and send messages to the printer to activate its various features.

Computer programs are like houses; living in a subdivision provides the most house for the dollar and can satisfy the most needs. In this chapter we have toured software suburbia: off-the-shelf programs that provide reliability and economy of scale. If your needs and your purse strings are greater, you have the option of hiring a contractor to create exactly what you want. With custom programs, as with custom homes, the job will take longer, cost more, and have more problems than anyone estimates. But you'll end up with exactly what you want.

There is yet another option: do it yourself. Unless you have a lot of experience, you probably shouldn't tackle a whole house, but you could probably handle a shed or some bookcases. Many computer users create simple programs that generate special forms, direct their printer to change fonts or spacing, or handle special tasks unique to their operation. You might prefer to pay a professional to do it, but as with hiring carpenters or plumbers, if you understand what they're doing, you're more likely to get what you want. With this in mind, let's shift our focus from programs to programming.

Common Software Terms

Applications software	Computer programs that are designed for specific tasks, such as word processing, data base management, and accounting.
Buffer	A portion of the computer's memory that is designated for a special purpose.
Communications program	Software that controls the process of transferring data from one computer to another.
Data base program	Software that controls assembly, storage, and manipulation of varied information in a structured format.
Disk emulator	A portion of the computer's memory that has been programmed to emulate a disk drive (also called electronic disk or RAM disk).
Integrated software	A collection of two or more programs that operate interdependently, can share data, and usually can be used without having to change disks.
Spooler	A portion of memory designated to store data for printing.
Spreadsheet program	Software that manipulates data in a ledger-style format and performs calculations from formulas stored in cells of the electronic "sheet."
Utilities	Programs that manage data operations and storage within the computer and on disks. DOS is a collection of utilities.
Word processing program	Software designed for entry, manipulation, and printing of text.

CHAPTER SEVEN

An Introduction to Programming and BASIC

For all its high-tech circuitry and attractive exterior, a computer is essentially a box that runs programs. And a program is just a set of instructions. When you set the bass, the treble, and the volume on your stereo, you are programming it. Programming is simply telling a stereo system, a computer, or a microwave oven what you want it to do.

Programs can get into the computer in several ways. They can be built into the computer, such as the Power-on Self-Test and the Cassette BASIC stored in the PC's ROM chips. They can also be purchased separately on disks, cassette tapes, or cartridges. Or you can type the program into the computer yourself. If you decide to type in a program, you can select one that was written by someone else. Many books and magazine articles include programs, and a few sample programs are included in this chapter. You can also develop your own programs.

For most purposes, the few programs in ROM plus the thousands of commercial programs available on disk are more than adequate. Although many PC users have never learned to program, they have never felt handicapped. But you may want to learn a little programming for at least four reasons: to have fun, to write useful programs, to get a better understanding of what computers and programs do and how they do it, and to enable you to communicate with programmers.

This chapter introduces you to programming in general and to programming in BASIC in particular. But it is only an introduction. After reading it and doing the exercises on your PC, you will be able to write simple programs. You will also have a good idea of what programming is and whether you want to pursue it further. If you do, you will be equipped to follow the many books and articles on BASIC. With a little more study, you will be able to take published program listings, type them into the computer, and make changes in them, either to experiment and learn or to adapt them to your needs.

Programming Languages

There are many programming languages. They all translate instructions from a form that the programmer understands into machine language, which the computer's hardware understands. Machine language instructions are made up of sequences of 0's and 1's, which represent "on" and "off," much like a light switch. Remember the game Twenty Questions? Instead of 1's and 0's, it is based on yes and no answers. With just 20 clues a good player can figure out almost any animal, mineral, or vegetable. Given a variety of combinations of 1's and 0's, an equally wide range of information can be communicated to the computer.

You don't have to talk to the computer in 1's and 0's, however. Programming languages were developed to enable computer users to give instructions to the computer more easily. A computer language is a translator; it takes a statement such as PRINT and translates it into a series of 1's and 0's that the computer can then execute.

But every programming language is different. Although BASIC understands PRINT, Pascal doesn't. Pascal's print instruction is WRITELN (short for "write line"). As with human languages, one computer language isn't better or worse than another—just different—and each one is suited to a different task. FORTRAN is the programming language of science because it is especially adept at handling complex equations (FORTRAN stands for "formula translation"). COBOL (an acronym for Common Business Oriented Language) is particularly good at searching through massive business files and telling the machine how to format complex forms, charts, and reports. Pascal (named after the seventeenth-century mathematician Blaise Pascal) has a very precise structure and is especially good for training serious programmers. BASIC was designed to be easy to learn and use (it stands for Beginners' All-Purpose Symbolic Instruction Code). One of BASIC's main drawbacks, however, is its slow execution speed.

Many languages are *compiled*. After you enter the lines of code, the entire program is translated into binary instructions (the

0's and 1's) and stored that way. Whenever you want to run the program, it's ready to go. BASIC is an *interpreted* language; the *source code* (original program) is stored, and each time the program is run it is translated and executed line by line. With a compiled program, the translation takes place only once—not every time you run the program. As you'll soon see, many programs contain loops, in which several instructions are executed over and over. In BASIC, if an instruction is carried out six times, it has to be translated six times. But you can compile a BASIC program to improve its execution speed by using a BASIC compiler.

Program Structures

In order for you to get an idea of programming, speed of execution isn't important. And for the short programs you are likely to write, speed isn't much of an issue. Remember the net worth program introduced in Chapter 2? The answers appeared on the screen the instant you pressed the <Enter> key. Let's look at that program again. This time, instead of Cassette BASIC, we'll use Disk BASIC.

Insert a copy of the DOS disk in drive A, turn on the machine or reboot, and when the A prompt appears type **BASIC** <Enter>. This command puts you in BASIC. Instead of the A prompt (or C if you're using an XT), you will see the BASIC prompt (Ok) on the screen. When you want to return to DOS, type **SYSTEM** <Enter>, and you'll see the DOS prompt on the screen.

Figure 7.1 shows what the screen might look like after you have entered and run a new version of the program. Notice that this time each line is preceded by a number. To test the program for yourself, type in lines 10 through 120, including the line numbers, and press <Enter> at the end of each line. Feel free to use capital letters, lowercase letters, or both. When you're finished, check the program for accuracy, and correct any errors using the cursor keys and the <Ins> and <Del> keys. (See the BASIC manual for a complete discussion of the BASIC editor.) Whenever you change a line, be sure to press <Enter> before moving to another line.

Now type **RUN** <Enter>, or simply press the <F2> key, and the computer will do it for you. The program creates and stores the variables named in the first four lines, does the computation asked for in the next line, then prints the result, '99100', on the screen. If you get a different number, you must have typed something in wrong. After displaying '99100', the PC then follows the instructions in the remaining lines, the last of which is to display the statement of net worth. When the program has finished running, the BASIC prompt reappears.

When you typed these instructions in Chapter 2, you omitted the line numbers, which made the computer execute each line as you entered it. This is known as direct mode, or calculator mode. It is

```
The IBM Personal Computer Basic
Version D2.00 Copyright IBM Corp. 1981, 1982, 1983
60894 Bytes free

Ok
10 HOMEVALUE = 86000
20 CARVALUE = 8000
30 FURNISHINGS = 5000
40 BANKACCOUNT 100
50 ASSETS = HOMEVALUE + CARVALUE + FURNISHINGS + BANKACCOUNT
60 PRINT ASSETS
70 MORTGAGE = 53000
80 CARLOAN = 4000
90 CREDITUNIONLOAN = 2000
100 LIABILITIES = MORTGAGE + CARLOAN + CREDITUNIONLOAN
110 PRINT LIABILITIES
120 PRINT "Net Worth Is $" ASSETS − LIABILITIES
RUN
 99100
 59000
Net Worth is $  40100
Ok

─

1LIST 2RUN◄ 3LOAD" 4SAVE" 5CONT◄6,"LPT1 7TRON◄8TROFF◄9KEY 0SCREEN
```

Figure 7.1 *A display of the net worth program in Disk BASIC.*

handy when you want to do a quick numerical calculation. In BASIC the symbols '+', '-', '*', and '/' are used to represent addition, subtraction, multiplication, and division, respectively. If, for example, you wanted to calculate 12 times 0.065 plus 3.14159 divided by 17, you could type

PRINT 12 * 0.065 + 3.14159/17 <Enter>

and the computer would perform the calculation and display the results. (The screen would respond with '.9647995'.) Like a scientific calculator, BASIC also has a variety of trigonometric, logarithmic, and other functions (these operations are discussed in the IBM BASIC manual).

Often, however, you will want to use the indirect mode, which requires line numbers and waits until you enter the RUN command before executing the instructions. Another feature of BASIC's indirect mode is retention of the current program in RAM until you erase it, replace it with another program, or turn off the computer. You can run a program many times without having to type it in each time. Try it: just press the <F2> key. (The function keys' operations in BASIC are displayed at the bottom of the screen whenever you are using the language.)

You can also store a program on disk by typing **SAVE"** followed by whatever file name you give the program—NETWORTH is as good as any (the file name must not include any spaces)—and then pressing <Enter>. (Pressing <F4> is another way to give the SAVE command.) Drive A will whir and light up while NETWORTH is being written on the disk.

When you wanted a directory of disk files in DOS, you typed **DIR.** In BASIC you type **FILES** <Enter>. The list should include NET-WORTH.BAS. As noted previously, the PC automatically adds the extension .BAS to BASIC files. Type **NEW** <Enter> to clear memory, then type **RUN** <Enter>. Since there is no program in memory, all you get is the Ok prompt. Now load the program into memory by typing **LOAD"NETWORTH** <Enter> (you don't have to type the .BAS extension). You can press <F3> instead of typing **LOAD"**. Now run the program. To examine the program again, type **LIST** <Enter> or <F1> <Enter>.

Notice that the commands in NETWORTH.BAS fall into three categories. Some commands enter data into the computer (CARVALUE = 8000), some process data that has already been entered (ASSETS = HOMEVALUE + CARVALUE + FURNISH-INGS + BANKACCOUNT), and some generate output (PRINT ASSETS). The operations within a program can be repeated, or the program can be structured so that certain operations will occur only when designated conditions are met. This versatility allows a programmer to build many options into a program while maintaining a program structure that is both orderly and efficient.

Iteration   NETWORTH.BAS executed each line in sequence. As mentioned previously, programs can *loop,* or repeat a series of instructions over and over. They can also make decisions, jumping to one set of instructions under one condition and to another set under another condition. Rather than writing actual programs to demonstrate these capabilities, let's create a pseudo-program. Because a program is simply a set of explicit instructions, you can simulate the form of a program without worrying about the details of syntax. For example, a program that tells a dishwasher to wash the dishes might go like this:

```
10 WASH
20 RINSE
30 WASH
40 RINSE
50 DRY
60 END
```

This program won't really run. Although BASIC understands PRINT, FILES, SAVE, and READ, as well as many other commands, it doesn't understand WASH or RINSE. But the logic is like that of a real program.

Instead of repeating the WASH and RINSE instructions twice, however, you could use BASIC's GOTO command:

```
10 WASH
20 RINSE
30 GOTO 10
40 DRY
50 END
```

The dishwasher will wash, rinse, and then loop back to line 10 and repeat the process indefinitely. The only problem is that it will continue to loop and never move on to line 40. If you ever get into an endless loop, press <Ctrl>-<Break> to stop the program. Since you want to go through the loop twice, you can use BASIC's FOR...NEXT commands to limit the number of repetitions:

```
10 FOR I = 1 TO 2
20     WASH
30     RINSE
40 NEXT I
50 DRY
60 END
```

Line 10 creates the variable I and sets it equal to 1. (I stands for "iteration" or "increment." You can use any variable you want, but I is conventional.) After the first wash and rinse, the computer changes I to 2 and repeats the process. Since 2 was as far as you told it to go, the program then moves to lines 50 and 60. To do more washing, you could have made line 10 read 'FOR I = 1 to 5', and the program would have gone through the loop five times. Indenting certain lines, such as those between a FOR and a NEXT, isn't required, but it makes the program easier to follow.

Decision What if you don't know how many times you want the program to loop? Instead of using a sequential or iterative structure, you can use one of BASIC's decision structures:

```
10 IF DISHES = CLEAN THEN GOTO 50
20 WASH
30 RINSE
40 GOTO 10
50 DRY
60 END
```

As long as DISHES are not CLEAN, the program will continue to loop through the WASH/RINSE sequence. As soon as DISHES are CLEAN, the program will DRY and END. (Although some versions of BASIC require that every program conclude with the END statement, in IBM BASIC it is optional.)

A blackjack program might use a similar conditional command structure:

```
120 IF (CARD1 + CARD2) = 21 THEN GOTO 190
     .
     .
     .
190 PRINT "BLACKJACK! CONGRATULATIONS, YOU WIN"
```

Besides comparing two sides of an equation for equality (as in the blackjack example above), BASIC can use '<', '>', '> =', '< =', and '<>', and carry out a specified action when one side is less than, greater than, greater than or equal to, less than or equal to, or not equal to the other side.

Input and Output

Each BASIC command is a logical building block, which a programmer uses to accomplish a certain task. The operations discussed so far deal with processing data. Before processing, however, the program has to provide a way for data to be entered (input), and after processing it has to pass the results out to the operator (output).

BASIC has three main instructions for entering data: LET, INPUT, and READ. You used the LET instruction in the NETWORTH program when you typed **HOMEVALUE = 86000**. Even though LET is missing from that instruction, IBM BASIC recognizes it as a LET statement. **HOMEVALUE = 86000** sets aside a location in memory, labels it 'HOMEVALUE', and stores the number 86000 in it.

If a program includes the INPUT instruction, it will pause at that point, print a question mark on the screen, and wait for you to enter the data from the keyboard. If you include a message in quotation marks in the command, the screen will display the message just before the question mark. Try this after clearing the computer's memory with the NEW command used earlier in the chapter:

```
10 INPUT "What is the value of your home?"; HOMEVALUE <Enter>
RUN <Enter>
```

The computer will display 'What is the value of your home? _'. Type **86000 <Enter>**. The number 86000 will be stored in a location labeled 'HOMEVALUE'. Now type **PRINT HOMEVALUE <Enter>**. The computer goes to the storage location, determines the value stored there, and displays '86000'.

That's fine if you want an interactive program, one in which the user enters the data when the program is run, but you may want to use the same information several times, without having to key it in each time. By using BASIC's DATA statement, you can store information in the program itself. Then the READ statement will make the program retrieve the stored data and work with it.

The DATA and READ statements are especially suited for word processing. Although you've been using numbers as examples of data, programs can process words just as easily. Most word processing programs are written in languages that operate faster than BASIC, but BASIC programs can also perform these tasks.

You've already used one of BASIC's output commands. The command PRINT causes whatever follows it to appear on the screen. If what follows is in quotes, it is displayed literally. Typing **PRINT "HOMEVALUE"** <Enter> will make the screen display 'HOME-VALUE'. If you omit the quotes, the program treats what follows as an instruction to retrieve a stored value or process data. Typing **PRINT HOMEVALUE** <Enter> will make the screen display '86000', and typing **PRINT 3 + 4** <Enter> will display '7'. The LPRINT statement works the same way, but it directs output to the printer instead of to the screen. (Make sure that the printer is on before running a program that includes this command.)

Graphics

If your PC is equipped with the IBM Color/Graphics Adapter or a comparable color board, you can easily write programs in BASIC to display a variety of pictures, diagrams, and graphs. Although a detailed discussion of graphics is beyond the scope of this book, let's take a brief look at some of the graphics features of BASIC. A PC with the Color/Graphics Adapter has three display modes: text mode, and medium- and high-resolution graphics modes. In text mode (also available on the IBM monochrome monitor) graphs are composed of the special block and line symbols available in the PC's character set. Text mode is useful for simple bar charts. The BASIC statements and functions used in text mode are CLS, COLOR, LOCATE, PRINT, WIDTH, WRITE, CSRLIN, POS, SCREEN, SPC, and TAB. In the medium-resolution graphics mode the screen is divided into a 320-column by 200-row grid. Each point (or *pixel,* for "picture element") on the screen can be one of four colors. In the high-resolution graphics mode the screen is divided into a 640-column by 200-row grid. Only two colors are possible in this mode.

A number of BASIC instructions make graphics easy in the medium- and high-resolution modes. The BASIC (and BASICA, or Advanced BASIC) instructions used with the graphics modes are CIRCLE, COLOR, DRAW, GET, LINE, PAINT, PRESET, PSET, PUT, SCREEN, and POINT. In the medium-resolution graphics mode the COLOR statement allows you to select the background color and one of two *palettes* of three foreground colors. The SCREEN statement may be used to change the display mode. The PSET and PRESET statements allow you to plot points by giving their coordinates. The LINE statement allows you to draw lines and rectangles.

```
10 ' Graphics demonstration program.  This program requires the
20 ' Color/Graphics Adapter and BASICA.
30 CLS
40 PRINT "Which palette would you like to use?"
50 PRINT "Palette 0  Palette 1"
60 PRINT " 1-green    1-cyan"
70 PRINT " 2-red      2-magenta"
80 PRINT " 3-brown    3-white"
90 INPUT "0 or 1";PALETTE
100 IF PALETTE<>0 AND PALETTE<>1 THEN 90
110 PRINT "Pick a background color."
120 PRINT "0-black     8-gray"
130 PRINT "1-blue      9-light blue"
140 PRINT "2-green    10-light green"
150 PRINT "3-cyan     11-light cyan"
160 PRINT "4-red      12-light red"
170 PRINT "5-magenta 13-light magenta"
180 PRINT "6-brown    14-yellow"
190 PRINT "7-white     15-bright white"
200 INPUT"Which color(0-15)";BACKCOLOR
210 IF BACKCOLOR<0 OR BACKCOLOR>15 THEN 200
220 CLS: KEY OFF
230 SCREEN 1,0 ' Select medium resolution graphics mode.
240 COLOR BACKCOLOR,PALETTE
250 LINE (1,1)-(318,198),1,B ' Draw a box.
260 CIRCLE (160,100),60,1 ' Draw circle
270 CIRCLE (160,100),80,3 '       "
280 CIRCLE (160,80),70,2 '        "
290 CIRCLE (160,120),70,3 '       "
300 CIRCLE (210,100),70,2 '       "
310 CIRCLE (110,100),70,3 '       "
320 FOR I=0 TO 318 STEP 4
330    LINE (1,0)-(I,199),1
340 NEXT
350 FOR DELAY=1 TO 3000:NEXT
360 LOCATE 24
370 INPUT "Again(y/n)";A$
380 IF A$="y" OR A$="Y" THEN RUN
390 END
```

Figure 7.2 *A program to demonstrate some of the PC's graphics capabilities.*

Advanced BASIC (BASICA) is required for a number of graphics statements such as CIRCLE (which is used for drawing circles), ellipses, and sectors (of circles). The PAINT statement can color a region of the screen. GET and PUT are used to store the graphics data from designated areas of the screen and display images that have been stored in that way. The DRAW statement enables you to draw figures using a graphics definition language. Using the command in this manner offers a convenient way to represent pictorial information.

If you have a Color/Graphics Adapter or another color graphics board, consult the BASIC manual, and experiment with these features. You'll be surprised at how easy it is to display graphics using BASIC. Let's look at the program shown in Figure 7.2, which uses some graphics features of BASIC and BASICA (you'll need BASICA and the Color/Graphics Adapter to run this program).

After typing in the program, proofread it for errors, and save it on disk. Try running the program a number of times, selecting a different palette and background color each time. Make sure that the background color you pick is not one of the colors in the palette, or the message 'Again (Y/N)?_' and any other text on the screen may not be visible. Study the program listing, and try to figure out how the program works. Consult the BASIC manual to see what the various statements do. Finally, try modifying the program to create a different display.

Sound

You can also use BASIC to output sound from the PC's internal speaker. The BEEP statement produces a tone at a frequency of 800 Hertz (Hz) for one-fourth of a second. This beeping sound, which is much like the tone generated by a telephone answering machine, can be used to attract the user's attention. The BEEP statement can also be used to indicate user errors or the completion of a process.

The SOUND statement is like the BEEP statement, except that you can specify the frequency and the duration of the tone. The SOUND statement makes the speaker produce a tone at a given frequency for a specified amount of time. The frequency is measured in Hertz (cycles per second); it must be between 37 and 32767 Hz. The amount of time is represented in terms of "ticks" of the PC's internal clock, which operates at 18.2 ticks per second.

A PLAY statement is available in Advanced BASIC. It allows you to generate music using a tune definition language with which you can specify octaves, tempo, musical notes, and other variables. Figure 7.3 is a simple program that demonstrates some of the SOUND features of BASIC and BASICA (the only statement that requires BASICA is the PLAY statement).

```
10 ' Sound demonstration program -- This program requires BASICA.
20 BEEP:PRINT "BEEP!"
30 FOR DELAY=1 TO 2000:NEXT: PRINT "Part of the PC's range. . ."
40 FOR I=40 TO 1400 STEP 10
50    SOUND I,.5
60 NEXT
70 FOR DELAY=1 TO 2000:NEXT: PRINT "Music. . ."
80 FOR I=1 TO 3
90    PLAY "CDEFGAB"
100 NEXT
110 PLAY "O5;C"
120 END
```

Figure 7.3 *A sample program to demonstrate some of the PC's sound capabilities.*

Syntax

Programming is input, processing, output, various modes of input and output, and various control structures that coordinate the whole operation. But, like spoken languages, computer languages involve more than form and structure; there are also syntax and the myriad details of spelling, punctuation, and grammar.

By now you've probably seen 'Syntax error' on the screen. If you haven't, type **Good day, PC** <Enter>. Instead of politely replying to your greeting, the machine will respond with some kind of syntax error. If you use the indirect mode, **10 Good day, PC** <Enter>, BASIC won't try to interpret your message until you type **RUN** <Enter>, at which time you will be confronted with a message such as 'Syntax error in 10'.

"Syntax error" covers a multitude of sins. If you enter something that doesn't fit BASIC's rules exactly, the computer won't know how to handle it. If you type **WASH**, you'll get a syntax error message. If you type **PRNT** when you mean **PRINT**, you'll get one also. Leaving out a space, adding a space, or forgetting a comma, a semicolon, or a quotation mark can also generate this message.

Although such messages can be frustrating, they are actually quite helpful. Imagine if such an error simply stopped the program. How would you go about locating the problem? Messages that tell you which line the errors are in make programming easier.

BASIC has more than 70 error messages. If you use FOR to set up a loop but forget its partner, NEXT, BASIC will print the message 'FOR without NEXT'. Try typing **LOAD"NETWIRTH** <Enter>. The computer won't say, 'Couldn't find it Boss, but there's a program here named NETWORTH; is that what you wanted?' But it will display 'File not found'. Consult the IBM BASIC manual for a list of all the error messages and their meanings. Don't let the number of error messages or the size of the BASIC manual scare you. Just as you don't need to be fluent in French to find the Louvre or order café au lait, you don't have to know all the details of BASIC to write a program. Start with a few instructions, and dive in. In most cases, you'll see what you did wrong right away and know how to correct it. And if you get an error message that you don't understand, look it up in the manual.

Sample Programs

To provide some practice, fun, and hints at what you can do with BASIC, let's try a one-line program, then add to it and experiment. While in BASIC, enter and run the following mini-program:

```
50 PRINT "Getting Started with the IBM PC and XT" <Enter>
```

Now put it into a loop. (Be sure to press <Enter> at the end of each line.)

```
30 FOR I = 1 TO 15
50 PRINT "Getting Started with the IBM PC and XT"
60 NEXT I
```

This program will print 'Getting Started with the IBM PC and XT' 15 times. That's a little more decorative, but printing all the lines at the left edge of the screen isn't very elegant. Use the LOCATE command to make the program begin printing at column 12, and use CLS to clear the screen so it displays only the new output:

```
20 CLS
30 FOR I = 1 TO 15
40      LOCATE, 12
50      PRINT "Getting Started with the IBM PC and XT"
60 NEXT I
```

Now you're getting somewhere. But putting each line directly over the other is still rather monotonous. If you change line 40 to **LOCATE, I + 12**, the first line will be in the same place, but each time the program goes through the loop, the text will begin one column to the right. In case you're reading this without a PC handy, Figure 7.4 shows the output from this final version of the program. Except for the Ok prompt, you've got a rather professional-looking display.

If you use the PRINT command alone, you'll get a blank line. If you give three PRINT commands, you can add three blank lines before the Ok. One way to do that is to add the following:

```
70 PRINT
80 PRINT
90 PRINT
```

You can put more than one command on a line by inserting colons between them. Add the following line to the program:

```
70 PRINT: PRINT: PRINT
```

You can also add a title to the program listing. If you start a line

```
                Getting Started with the IBM PC and XT
              Getting Started with the IBM PC and XT
             Getting Started with the IBM PC and XT
            Getting Started with the IBM PC and XT
           Getting Started with the IBM PC and XT
          Getting Started with the IBM PC and XT
         Getting Started with the IBM PC and XT
        Getting Started with the IBM PC and XT
       Getting Started with the IBM PC and XT
      Getting Started with the IBM PC and XT
     Getting Started with the IBM PC and XT
    Getting Started with the IBM PC and XT
   Getting Started with the IBM PC and XT
  Getting Started with the IBM PC and XT
 Getting Started with the IBM PC and XT

Ok
—
```

Figure 7.4 *Output from the sample program (listed in text) to display this book's title.*

```
10 REM PROGRAM TO PRINT A BANNER
20 CLS
30 FOR I = 1 TO 15
40      LOCATE, I + 12
50      PRINT "Getting Started with the IBM PC and XT"
60 NEXT I
70 PRINT: PRINT: PRINT
80 END
```

Figure 7.5 *A sample program to display a banner.*

with REM or an apostrophe, the computer will treat the line as a remark and won't try to execute it. Scattered remarks throughout a program can serve as internal documentation. Finish the program by adding an END statement. Figure 7.5 shows the complete program listing.

After you have tried this program, experiment with it. (First save it on disk by typing **SAVE"BANNER** <Enter>.) Write your own banner message for line 50, vary the number of PRINT commands in line 70, and try changing the numbers in line 30. Look up the complete syntax for the LOCATE statement in the BASIC manual, and try modifying line 40.

Type in the program shown in Figure 7.6, and then use the SAVE command to store it on disk. Although the program includes a number of new BASIC commands, you don't have to understand

```
1000 ' Guess 1.00 -- A simple guessing game
1010 RANDOMIZE VAL(RIGHT$(TIME$,2)) ' Initialize random number generator.
1020 MAX=100 ' Set the largest number the computer can pick.
1030 TRIES=10 ' Set the number of tries the user gets.
1040 KEY OFF ' Turn off the function key list at the bottom of the screen.
1050 CLS ' Clear the screen.
1060 SOUND 300,6 ' Sound tone.
1070 PRINT:PRINT "I'm thinking of a number from 1 to"STR$(MAX)"."
1080 PRINT "You will have"TRIES"tries to guess the number."
1090 PRINT "I will tell you whether your guess is too high or too low.
1100 PRINT
1110 INPUT "How many games would you like to play";GAMES
1120 WINS=0
1130 FOR NUMBEROFGAMES=1 TO GAMES
1140    NUMBER=INT(RND(1)*MAX)+1 ' Pick a random number.
1150    PRINT "I've picked a number."
1160    TURN=1
1170    WHILE NUMBER<>GUESS AND TURN<=TRIES
1180      INPUT"What is your guess";GUESS
1190      IF GUESS<=MAX AND GUESS>=1 THEN 1220
1200      PRINT "You must choose a number between 1 and"STR$(MAX)"."
1210      GOTO 1180
1220      IF GUESS>NUMBER THEN PRINT "That number is too big."
1230      IF GUESS<NUMBER THEN PRINT "That number is too small."
1240      TURN=TURN+1
1250    WEND
1260    IF GUESS=NUMBER THEN PRINT "You won!":WINS=WINS+1:GOTO 1280
1270    PRINT "Sorry.  That's"TRIES"guesses.  The number was"STR$(NUMBER)"."
1280 NEXT
1290 PRINT "You have won"WINS;
1300 IF WINS=1 THEN PRINT "game "; else PRINT "games ";
1310 PRINT "out of"games"played."
1320 INPUT "Would you like to play again";Q$
1330 IF LEFT$(Q$,1)="y" OR LEFT$(Q$,1)="Y" THEN 1060
1340 BEEP:PRINT "Bye!":END
```

Figure 7.6 *A guessing game
to match numbers with the
computer.*

any of them to enter the program and use it. You can now copy and
use any published BASIC program intended for the PC. But if you
want to customize a program or convert one written for a different
version of BASIC so it will run on the PC, you'll need to understand
what each statement does. Start with the checklist following this
chapter, and then use the BASIC manual or a book on BASIC.

Tips for Using BASIC

■ Use meaningful variable names. You can use up to 40 characters as long as there are no spaces between them.

■ Use plenty of remarks. Give each program a title, and insert explanations for each section of your program. BASIC allows a handy shortcut: instead of the letters REM, you can precede each remark with an apostrophe.

■ Another shortcut is to use the <Alt> key to print certain BASIC key words on the screen. Simply pressing <Alt>-P causes PRINT to be displayed, <Alt>-G displays GOTO, and so on. An especially handy one is <Alt>-A, for AUTO. AUTO <Enter> causes line numbers to appear automatically as you type each line. When you've typed the last line, <Ctrl>-<Break> turns off the line numbering function.

■ One of the best ways to improve your BASIC skills is to read programs that appear in various books and magazines. Even if many of the commands are foreign to you, you will begin to spot loops and other standard structures. As with learning any language, you will quickly become familiar with other items as you progress.

A Quick Reference to BASIC Commands*

Command	Syntax	Example	Result
CLS	CLS	CLS	Clears the screen; leaves memory undisturbed.
DATA	DATA constant [,constant]...	DATA 86000, 8000	Stores information in file; see READ.
END	END	END	Terminates program's execution.
FILES	FILES	FILES \<Enter\>	Displays a list of files in the current drive; similar to DOS command DIR/W.
FOR...NEXT	FOR variable = x TO y NEXT variable	FOR I = 1 TO 5 PRINT "Hello" NEXT I	Sets up a loop; commands between these lines are repeated until I reaches the number indicated.
GOTO	GOTO line	GOTO 80	Causes the program to jump to the line specified.
IF...THEN... ELSE	IF expression [,] THEN clause [ELSE clause]	IF X\<=0 THEN GOTO 60 PRINT "X is positive"	If the condition is true, the program does one thing; if false, it does another; the word ELSE is optional.

*The syntax presented for each command covers only the usage presented in this chapter. Some of the commands permit additional variations, which are presented in the IBM BASIC manual.

Command	Syntax	Example	Result
INPUT	INPUT[;]["prompt";] variable	INPUT X	Program displays "?" and pauses; number entered from keyboard is assigned to variable X.
LEFT$	V$ = LEFT$(x$,n)	X$ = "IBM PC & XT" V$ = LEFT(X$,3)	Takes the three leftmost characters (IBM) and assigns them to V$.
LET	[LET] variable = expression	LET X = 5	Assigns a value to a variable; can also be written without the word LET, as X = 5.
LIST	LIST	LIST <Enter> or F1 <Enter>	Displays the program currently in memory on the screen.
LOAD	LOAD filespec	LOAD"program1 <Enter> or F3 <Enter>	Retrieves program from disk.
LOCATE	LOCATE [row][,[col]]	LOCATE 5, 10	Places the cursor at the location indicated, in this case row 5, column 10.
LPRINT	LPRINT [list of expressions]	LPRINT X	Causes printer to print the value of X; if no value has been assigned, prints 0.
		LPRINT "X"	Causes printer to print the character X.
NEW	NEW	NEW <Enter>	Clears the current program from memory; used prior to typing in a new program. Not needed prior to loading a program from disk, since LOAD automatically clears memory.
PRINT	PRINT [list of expressions]	PRINT X	Displays the value of X on the screen; if no value has been assigned, displays 0.
		PRINT "X"	Displays the character X on the screen.
		PRINT	Creates a blank line in the screen display.
RANDOMIZE	RANDOMIZE [n]	RANDOMIZE 1664	Reseeds random number generator.
READ	READ variable [,variable]...	READ homevalue, carvalue	Retrieves information from a file and assigns it to variables listed; see DATA.

Command	Syntax	Example	Result
REM	REM remark	REM This is a remark.	Creates a remark, a line that is ignored by BASIC.
RIGHT$	V$ = RIGHT$(x$,n)	X$ = "IBM PC & XT" V$ = RIGHT(X$,2)	Takes the two rightmost characters (XT) and assigns them to V$.
RND	V = RND	V = RND	Generates a random number between 0 and 1 and assigns it to V; will generate the same number or series of numbers each time unless RANDOMIZE is used.
RUN	RUN	RUN <Enter> or F2	Executes the program currently in memory.
SAVE	SAVE filespec	SAVE"program1 <Enter> or F4 program1 <Enter>	Stores the program currently on disk.
SYSTEM	SYSTEM	SYSTEM <Enter>	Leaves BASIC and returns to DOS.

Hardware for the PC and XT

In Chapter 1 we toured the PC's hardware. I likened it to a half-day bus tour of a new city—adequate for orientation, but not enough time to relax in the bistros or wander the museums. We took a similar tour of software in Chapter 6. Now it's time to return to the hardware, but more selectively and in greater depth.

Perhaps the most significant feature of the IBM PC is that it is an open system. IBM is usually quite security conscious, carefully guarding the details of its technology. Yet when the PC was released, IBM chose to let the world in on the computer's secrets. Except for the instructions contained in the ROM chips, IBM declared the whole system fair game and published technical specifications for virtually every element of the PC.

This strategy led to the development of a multimillion-dollar industry. Manufacturers from Bellevue, Washington, to Cassleberry, Florida, began producing a variety of components for the PC that could never have been conceived of had IBM kept the PC a closed system. As a result, there is not simply one PC, but a variety of possible PC systems. IBM itself calls its several PC configurations a family and includes PCjr in the group.

You can turn your PC into almost anything you want. If you're not satisfied with a keyboard for inputting data, you can choose from a variety of joysticks, light pens, optical readers, touch pads, mice, or even voice recognition devices. If you want more RAM, more disk capacity, or additional features, they are all readily available. Here are some of them.

Memory

The heart of IBM's PC family is the Intel 8088, 16-bit microprocessor chip. Actually, only part of the 8088 uses 16-bit architecture. The data bus, which is to a chip what a port is to a computer —an input/output pathway—is only 8 bits wide; it cannot process information as fast as chips that employ a 16-bit bus.

More important than bus size, however, is memory address size. An 8-bit chip can address only 64K of memory locations at one time, so most 8-bit computers are limited to 64K of RAM. A few expand memory by using two or more banks of 64K and switching between them. While this procedure allows them access to 128K or more, it is cumbersome and limiting.

The 8088 can address a full megabyte (1024K) of memory. The PC allocates some of it to ROM, some to the monitor, and some to other purposes, leaving 640K as the maximum that is usable at one time. That is ten times the memory available in most 8-bit computers.

Since the PC comes with 64K, and the XT with 128K, why not just leave well enough alone? You might want more RAM to run larger programs. More program features demand more memory; some of the most complex and powerful applications programs cannot operate on a 64K machine. And each new version of DOS takes up more space in memory than its predecessor. In DOS 1.10, for example, COMMAND.COM used 4959 bytes of RAM, while its counterpart in DOS 2.00 requires 17,664 bytes. A number of programs that could run on a 64K machine with DOS 1.10 require a minimum of 128K when they are used in conjunction with DOS 2.00.

Because PC systems that have more memory are becoming increasingly common, a number of software companies have added features to their programs, thus increasing the programs' size. Version 2.3 of *dBASE II*, for example, operated on a 96K PC, whereas version 2.4 requires 128K. Many newer programs have been designed from the ground up to take advantage of greater memory capacity. You cannot run either *MBA* (Context Management Systems) or *ThinkTank* (Living Videotext), to cite two examples, unless your PC or XT has been upgraded to at least 256K.

More memory also means more data-handling capability. Many programs can work with only as much data as you can hold in RAM at one time.

Extra RAM also enables you to partition the computer's memory into two or more segments that can be used for different purposes, such as a printing buffer (as discussed in Chapter 6). Partitioning memory in this way allows the printer to receive data from the buffer while the computer performs other activities.

A segment of RAM can also serve as a disk emulator (also discussed in Chapter 6). For example, my PC has 512K of RAM: 256K on the system board and 256K on a plug-in board. Of the 512K, 360K is designated as drive C, which emulates a floppy disk drive but operates at far greater speed. The one hazard of a disk emulator, however, is that its contents can be wiped out by a power interruption, so you must frequently copy the data to a floppy disk drive.

When you examined the system board in Chapter 1, you saw one or more sets of nine chips each, with enough room for a total of four sets. This four-row arrangement allows the system boards in earlier PCs, which used 16K chips, to hold a total of 64K of RAM; later PC system boards, which use 64K chips, can hold 256K of RAM. Beyond these limits, additional RAM is contained on separate plug-in boards (or cards).

Plug-in Boards

Every PC or XT has a display adapter board in one of its expansion slots. Every XT, and almost every PC, has a floppy disk controller card. (A few PCs were sold without disk drives; they use a cassette recorder to store programs and data. This option never caught on, however.) XTs also have a hard disk controller card and an asynchronous (serial) card. That leaves three empty slots in the PC (out of a total of five) and four in the XT (out of eight).

Besides using these slots for extra memory, you can use them for additional ports or functions. Even if you have one serial port, you might want another, perhaps to connect a letter quality printer, a mouse, or an external modem to the computer. The IBM adapter for the monochrome monitor includes a parallel port for a printer, but the Color/Graphics Adapter doesn't, and you need a parallel port to connect most printers to the PC or the XT.

If you add all these options to your system, you could run out of expansion slots very quickly. The usual solution to this problem is to take advantage of the many multifunction boards on the market. You can buy a single board that includes 384K of RAM (which, added to 256K on your system board, brings the computer to its 640K maximum), a parallel port, a game port, two serial ports, and a clock. Another possible solution is purchasing an auxiliary expansion chassis such as the IBM Expansion Unit, which provides a 10-megabyte hard disk (with its own power supply) and eight additional expansion slots.

Monitors

Figure 8.1 illustrates the display options supported by IBM. You can use the IBM Monochrome Display and Printer Adapter with the IBM monochrome monitor, or the IBM Color/Graphics Adapter with the IBM color monitor. You can also connect a non-IBM color monitor, a TV, or a monitor capable of displaying graphics and text in one color to the IBM Color/Graphics Adapter. Several independent manufacturers produce adapters that enable the PC to display graphics on either a color monitor or a non-IBM monochrome monitor; some adapters even provide graphics on the IBM monochrome monitor.

The IBM monochrome monitor provides detailed, flicker-free text. But in addition to generating letters, numbers, and the various punctuation and symbols shown on the keyboard, the IBM Monochrome Display and Printer Adapter board can generate a wide range of shapes that can be combined into borders, block diagrams, bar graphs, and the like. They are called character graphics, block graphics, or line graphics, depending on which symbols are used. Figure 8.2 illustrates examples of these symbols. (The IBM Color/Graphics Adapter can also generate these symbols.)

The PC's monochrome board cannot generate either color or high-resolution graphics, but the Color/Graphics Adapter in conjunction with a color TV or a color monitor can. Unlike paint or crayons, whose primary colors are red, yellow, and blue, the primary colors that make up a video image are red, green, and blue. The Color/Graphics Adapter sends these colors as three separate signals to the 9-pin D-connector on the back of the Color/Graphics Adapter. By plugging an RGB (red, green, blue) monitor into this connector, the three colors are sent separately and are then combined by the monitor for the best possible color and resolution. (The IBM color monitor is an RGB monitor.) Yet even with the Color/Graphics Adapter and the highest quality RGB monitor, text is not as detailed as on the IBM monochrome monitor used with the adapter made for it.

In addition to sending separate red, green, and blue signals to an RGB monitor, the Color/Graphics Adapter can send a combined signal to a color TV, a color monitor designed to take only this *composite* signal, or a non-IBM monochrome monitor. Each of these alternatives has limitations compared to the two IBM monitors. The composite color monitor, while less expensive than an RGB monitor, does not produce a picture as clear as the RGB's, and it is usually limited to displaying 40 characters of text, as opposed to the standard 80-character width. A TV requires an adapter, the RF modulator, and has the lack of clarity of a composite monitor. A non-IBM monochrome monitor can display images generated by the Color/

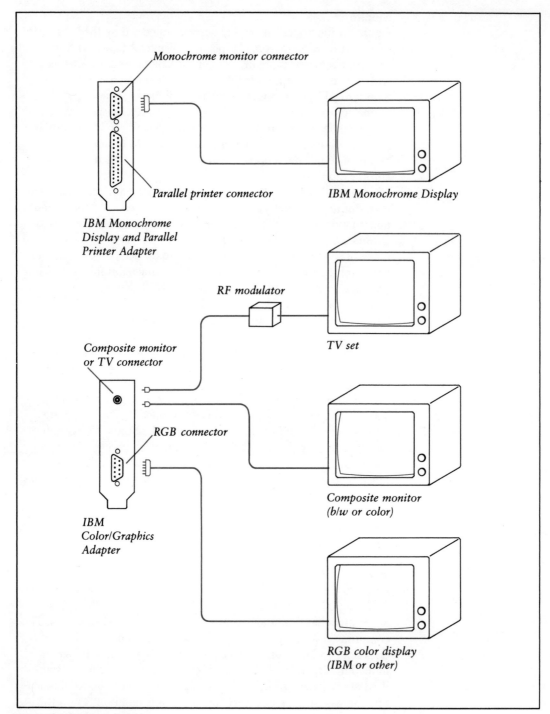

Monochrome monitor connector

Parallel printer connector

IBM Monochrome Display

IBM Monochrome
Display and Parallel
Printer Adapter

RF modulator

TV set

Composite monitor
or TV connector

RGB connector

IBM
Color/Graphics
Adapter

Composite monitor
(b/w or color)

RGB color display
(IBM or other)

Figure 8.1 *Options for using
monitors and adapters for
the PC and XT.*

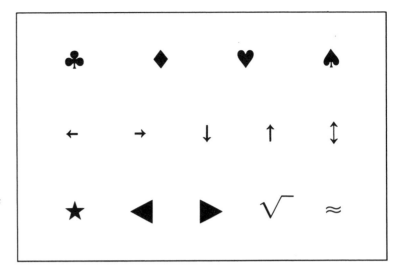

Figure 8.2 *Selected graphics characters that can be displayed on the PC and XT, represented here by a type-setter's symbols.*

Graphics Adapter but in only one color, and its text is not as crisp as that of the IBM monochrome monitor.

One advantage of the TV-RF modulator combination is that except for the inexpensive modulator, it requires no additional cash outlay. This combination is adequate for games and limited other uses, but for serious or extended computing, you should choose one of the other options.

Because both the PC and the XT have expansion slots, you can plug in both adapter boards and connect a monochrome screen to one (for text) and a color screen to the other (for graphics). You can even use them simultaneously if your software is designed for this purpose, or you can switch between them to suit the task at hand. But this approach requires that you devote two expansion slots to display generation, which may leave you short on room for other options.

Some manufacturers offer a multidisplay board that emulates both IBM adapters on a single board and provides connectors in back that allow you to hook up a color monitor, a TV, or the IBM monochrome monitor. Although you can use only one monitor at a time, by using such a board you can switch between them easily.

Other manufacturers offer boards that emulate the IBM Mono-chrome Display and Printer Adapter but also have graphics capability (without color). These boards enable you to create graphics on your PC, and they display the graphics generated by some, but not all, applications programs that use graphics.

Modems

A modem is a device that translates computer signals into pulses that can be sent over telephone lines. With the aid of a communications program, it is used to swap data between your system and another computer. *Modem* is a combination of the words *modulator* and *demodulator*, the technical terms for the signal-translation process. The two main considerations in choosing a modem are transmission speed (*baud rate*) and whether to buy an internal or an external modem. (See Figure 8.3 for examples of modem types.)

A modem's baud rate is simply the speed (the number of bits per second) at which it can send data. Modems that operate at 300 baud can transmit approximately 30 characters per second (cps), while those rated at 1200 baud can transmit about 120 cps. Most 1200-baud modems can switch to 300 baud when a slower speed is desirable.

As you might guess, more speed costs more money, so the choice is not clear-cut. If you expect to transmit large quantities of

Figure 8.3 *Three types of modems: acoustic and direct-connect models, which are external to the PC, and a plug-in modem, which fits into one of the PC's expansion slots.*

Acoustic modem

Direct-connect modem

data or use long-distance phone lines, a 1200-baud modem is a good investment. If your data transmission needs are more modest, you can buy a 300-baud modem at one-third the price.

Three or four years ago most modems were *acoustic*. This type of modem has two rubber cups into which you place the telephone handset. Because the connection between the handset and the modem's cups does not always prevent interference from surrounding noise, transmission errors can occur with an acoustic modem. Today, most modems used with both the PC and the XT are *direct-connect* modems, which have standard modular phone jacks instead of rubber cups; you just plug the phone line into the jack and use the modem. (If you don't have a telephone with a modular jack, you will have to use an acoustic modem.)

Acoustic modems are external; they are located ouside the PC system unit. Most direct-connect modems are also external. Whether acoustic or direct-connect, an external modem takes up space and must be connected to the computer's serial port by a cable.

You can also buy a modem for the PC or the XT that is entirely contained on a plug-in board. Put this board into one of the computer's expansion slots, plug the phone into a jack on the rear of the board (which is flush with the back of the PC), and you're all set.

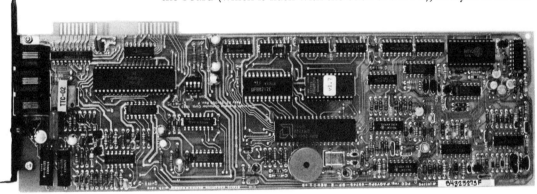

Plug-in modem

Internal modems have the advantage of being out of sight and out of the way—no box, no extra cable. They also may cost a little less because they do not require a separate serial port (an external modem requires a serial port to connect it to the computer). But if you already have a serial port (as part of a multifunction board, for example), an external modem has the advantage of not using one of those precious slots. If you're sure you won't run out of slots for other plug-in boards, you may be happier with an internal modem. But if you ever need to plug in another board and run out of slots, you will definitely be happier with the external variety.

As you recall from Chapter 6, a modem functions in conjunction with communications software. Many modems include a program in the purchase price. A number of separate programs are also available. You should verify that a communications program will operate properly with the modem you have or plan to purchase.

Printers

In choosing a system, most people emphasize the computer and the software. Choosing a printer is frequently an afterthought. In some respects the printer is the most critical part of the system. What it produces is the image you present to the world. It is also a potential bottleneck. For your PC or XT to operate at peak efficiency, the

Figure 8.4 *Examples of text and graphics produced by three types of printers and a plotter.*

```
                                           April 1, 1984

     Edgar Foote, Editor
     IQ Magazine
     P. O. Box 456
     New York, New York  10001

     Dear Mr. Foote:

     Thank you for your prompt reply to my suggestions for an article
     entitled "Using a Computer to Determine Your IQ."  I will send
     the manuscript to you within two weeks.

                                    Cordially,

                                    Ernest Hand
```

Dot matrix printer

```
                                           April 1, 1984

     Edgar Foote, Editor
     IQ Magazine
     P. O. Box 456
     New York, New York  10001

     Dear Mr. Foote:

     Thank you for your prompt reply to my suggestions for an article
     entitled "Using a Computer to Determine Your IQ."  I will send
     the manuscript to you within two weeks.

                                    Cordially,

                                    Ernest Hand
```

Letter quality printer

Ink jet printer

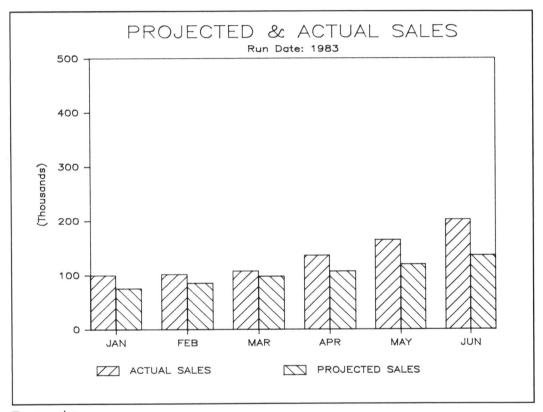

Two-pen plotter

printer should receive the proper consideration, connection, control, and care.

Printing text   Dot matrix printers are fast, inexpensive, and provide hard copy that generally looks like it came from a computer (a series of dots that make up the shape of a letter or a symbol). For casual letters or internal reports, dot matrix text is probably acceptable, but for material intended for clients or customers, the effect can be much the same as if you showed up for an appointment in jeans and a sweatshirt. If making the best impression is important, you'll want a letter quality printer, which uses a daisy wheel or a thimble to produce fully formed characters like those produced by a typewriter.

Recently, the text produced by dot matrix printers has improved and letter quality printers have become less expensive. So acquiring a printer—or even two—is not the economic burden it used to be. A few years ago the most inexpensive letter quality printers cost more than $2000; today you can buy one at somewhere between $600 and $1000. The lower priced letter quality printers are slow, however, printing between 12 and 20 cps. Dot matrix printers selling for half as much can crank out text at 80 to 160 cps.

Some businesses have one of each. Employees don't have to twiddle their thumbs for 45 minutes while a draft of a production report slowly appears, but they can print letters and final reports with typewriter-quality text.

If you can get by with good, but not perfect, type quality, you might consider a multispeed dot matrix printer that provides correspondence-quality print. These printers can turn out drafts at high speed, then slow down, squeeze more dots into each letter, and produce printing that falls only a little short of true letter quality. (See Figure 8.4 for examples of text produced by the commonly used printers.)

For strictly personal use, *thermal printers* are generally the least expensive, but they require special paper and often produce low-quality print. *Ink jet printers,* once priced in the stratosphere, are now becoming affordable. These printers can offer the best of both worlds—top speed and top quality. And ink jet printers are quieter than both dot matrix and letter quality printers. In fact, they make less noise than an XT's hard disk. Aside from price, which still tends to be higher than most other printers for comparable quality, the only serious drawback is an inability to handle multiform carbons.

Printing graphics   So far, this discussion of printers has focused on printing text. Graphics are another matter, and as usual, there are trade-offs. Most dot matrix printers can print graphics, though slowly and often with only moderate detail. Ink jet printers can do a better job with graphics, but at a higher price.

For serious graphics applications, *plotters* have the advantage of actually drawing lines, not just assembling tiny dots. Plotters use two or more small pens to form lines and characters; they move both the pens and the paper inside the printer to produce images in a variety of colors. They provide true curves, and their multiple pens

	Speed	Cost	Text Quality	Graphics	Color
Dot Matrix	Fast	Low	Fair to very good	Fair	Fair*
Letter Quality (daisy wheel or thimble)	Slow	Medium	Excellent	Limited	Limited
Ink Jet	Medium to very fast	Medium to high	Good to excellent	Fair to excellent	Excellent*
Plotter	Slow	Medium	Fair	Yes	Excellent

*Color available on more expensive models.

Figure 8.5 *Comparative features of three types of printers and a plotter.*

deliver excellent color rendition. But plotters have only limited text printing capability, and because they draw each letter separately, much as you or I would, they can be torturously slow. (Figure 8.5 presents a summary of the features of commonly used printers.)

Hard Disks

Hard disks (also called fixed disks) may be either an extravagant luxury or an economical necessity, depending on your intended use of the PC or XT system. Although most people find floppy disks adequate, hard disks provide two important advantages over floppy disks: greater storage capacity and greater speed. Whereas a standard double-sided floppy disk for the PC or the XT can store a maximum of 360K, even the smallest hard disk can hold 5 megabytes (about 5000K). Hard disk drives available for the PC range from 5 to 40 megabytes in capacity. Data transfer rates for hard disk drives are much faster than for their floppy counterparts; it is not unusual for a hard disk drive to read and write data 10 to 20 times faster than a floppy disk drive.

A hard disk drive may be mounted either inside the PC system unit or externally in a cabinet or expansion unit. The XT, for example, has an internally mounted 10-megabyte hard disk drive. IBM also offers an external Expansion Unit that has a 10-megabyte hard disk drive for either the PC or the XT. A number of other companies offer a variety of internal and external hard disk drives for the PC.

Most of the internally mounted hard disk drives for the PC (although not for the XT) require an external power supply. (If your hard disk is externally mounted or has an external power supply, you should turn on the hard disk's power switch before you turn on the PC system unit.) Although installing an internal hard disk drive isn't difficult, you may wish to have your dealer install it for you.

Included with a hard disk drive is a hard disk controller card and often some software. The hard disk controller is much like the floppy disk controller; it consists of a board and the cables needed to attach the hard disk to the PC. The controller card must be plugged into one of the PC expansion slots, whether the hard disk is installed internally or externally. (The controller card is supplied with the XT.)

Unless you have software that cannot otherwise work with a hard disk, you should generally use DOS 2.00 or a later version; earlier versions of DOS (1.00 and 1.10) can support hard disks only if they have nonstandard modifications. Such modifications to DOS invariably result in compatibility problems with certain software.

Some hard disk drives run under DOS 2.00 without any special software; others require specially written additions to DOS called *device drivers*. If a hard disk drive requires device drivers, this software should come with the disk drive. Once you have successfully installed and formatted a hard disk drive, however, it generally doesn't matter whether you are using the hard disk device drivers supplied with DOS 2.00 or those supplied with your hard disk.

Floppy disks have the curse and the blessing of being removable. Although it's great to exchange disks with another PC user or accumulate a library of disks, it's easy to forget what is on which disk and get lost in the floppy shuffle. Hard disks come in two varieties: fixed and removable. Most hard disks, such as the ones marketed by IBM, are fixed—the disk itself is sealed permanently inside the disk drive. With fixed disks, you needn't worry about touching the wrong part of the disk or inserting the disk carelessly, although you must be very careful when handling or moving the drive because it has such an intricate internal mechanism.

The capacity of a fixed disk drive is finite, whereas you can store an unlimited amount of information on a floppy disk drive by replacing each full disk with an empty one. Of course, with 5 or more megabytes of available storage space, it may be quite some time before you run out of space on a fixed disk drive.

Even in a system with the flexibility of one or more floppy drives, it may be desirable to have a removable hard disk. A number of companies are marketing hard disk drives for the PC that store information on removable hard disk cartridges. These disk drives effectively solve the two major problems associated with fixed disk drives: running out of space and making backup copies of hard disk files.

Unfortunately, however, if you want to exchange disk cartridges with other owners of removable hard disks, you may run into problems unless the information on the cartridges was written using the same brand of disk drive and device drivers. Compatibility problems result from the lack of a standard format for removable cartridges. Although most removable cartridges are one of two types (5.25 inches and 3.9 inches), the software supplied with one brand of disk drive may format the cartridge in such a way that the software supplied with another brand may not be able to read it.

Hard disk drives from sources other than IBM come in a variety of shapes and sizes. Some are packaged in a box that looks similar to the PC system unit; others are not packaged at all and must be installed inside the PC system unit. Some include a digital tape backup device; others do not. One popular model contains two 3.9-inch removable hard disk cartridges. The technical differences between the IBM hard disk drives and those from other manufacturers are, for the most part, unimportant as long as the drives work with DOS 2.00 or later versions. One difference between IBM hard disk drives and most others is that using the IBM drives (in the XT), you can boot the system from a hard disk. Using other drives, you must first load DOS from a floppy disk before being able to use the hard disk.

The XT and the Expansion Unit

Although the XT differs from the standard PC in several ways, the most obvious difference is that the XT comes with an internally mounted 10-megabyte fixed disk drive. Whereas the standard PC has five expansion slots, the XT has eight (although two of these will accommodate only short boards). The eight expansion slots in the XT are situated somewhat closer together than the five slots in the standard PC; for this reason, boards designed for the PC may require a different mounting bracket to be installed in the XT. A few boards, particularly those with piggyback attachments, may not even fit into the XT's cramped space between the expansion slots.

The XT has a much larger power supply to support the hard disk and the additional expansion slots. The XT lacks a cassette port, although that omission should not prove much of an inconvenience. The only software needed to run the XT's hard disk drive is DOS 2.00 (or a later version). All software developed for the PC will also run on the XT, although many programs that cannot be copied must always be loaded from the floppy drive.

Although the expansion potential of the PC is considerable, two limitations are the power supply and the number of expansion slots. The power supply in the PC is not vigorous enough to support a standard hard disk drive, and each slot is a precious commodity. The IBM Expansion Unit provides a satisfactory—though expensive—solution to this dilemma if you have a PC and don't want to duplicate your system by purchasing an XT. The Expansion Unit comes in two versions: one for the PC and one for the XT. Both contain 10-megabyte hard disks; the only difference is that the one for the PC includes the hard disk controller board. This board comes packaged inside the XT and can control two fixed disks; thus it is not included in the XT Expansion Unit.

The Expansion Unit looks just like a PC or an XT system unit, and like the XT system unit, the Expansion Unit provides eight expansion slots. The power supply can support two hard disk drives mounted inside the unit. If you are using an Expansion Unit with an XT, you or your dealer will have to install the XT's hard disk drive and controller board in the Expansion Unit. This relocation is necessary because the controller board must be in the same chassis as the drives it supports. The IBM Expansion Unit gives the owner of a PC all the capabilities of an XT, although three more slots are available in an XT attached to an Expansion Unit than in a PC attached to an Expansion Unit.

Take Your Time

When you order a new car, your choices don't end with the particular make. You still have to decide on the model, the color, the upholstery, and the accessories. Then after driving it a while, you may wish to add things that hadn't previously occurred to you. In a sense, you get to create your own car.

In the same sense, you can create your own PC or XT. The range of available hardware options when you purchase your PC or want to expand it later is greater than for any other computer system ever produced. Resist the temptation to get carried away by this flexibility. Analyze your needs, and add only the hardware that your work requires. Microcomputer technology is advancing rapidly, and prices are generally falling. Judicious hardware choices will give you a useful, economical, and still-expandable PC or XT system.

Common Hardware Terms

Baud rate A measurement of the speed at which data travels, commonly used for transmissions over modems.

Composite monitor A television or other monitor that receives all color signals in one stream of data.

Dot matrix printer A printer that produces characters and graphics symbols by arranging patterns of dots on paper.

Ink jet printer A printer that produces characters and graphics symbols by sending ink through one or more small jets that move to form the shape of the desired images.

Joystick A cursor control device commonly used with games.

Letter quality printer A printer that produces characters, and a limited selection of graphics symbols, in a manner similar to that of a typewriter.

Modem A device that converts a computer's digital signals into analog pulses for transmission over telephone lines, and vice versa. An acoustic modem has a cradle that holds the telephone receiver, and a direct-connect modem attaches directly to a modular telephone line.

Mouse A hand-held device that controls the cursor and allows limited command input to the computer. The mouse has begun to gain acceptance as an alternatve to the keyboard and can make computer use inviting and easy.

Plotter   A printer that uses one or more pens to form solid lines on paper. Plotters are widely used for reproducing simple graphics made up of straight and curved lines.

RF modulator   A device that converts computer signals for display on a television screen.

RGB monitor   A monitor that accepts separate signals for data to be displayed in red, green, and blue. An RGB monitor generally produces higher quality color images than a TV or other composite monitor (which can accept only a combined signal rather than separate ones).

Getting Started with a Hard Disk

Computer terms often seem like the arcane tongue of an extra-terrestrial species. Yet any specialized field has its own language, and in the long run these terms improve communication. But when a field is as new and rapidly changing as the world of personal computers, we may not have assimilated yesterday's coinage before today's turns up. Take, for example, the fast, large-capacity, non-removable disk drives discussed in the previous chapter. At first they were dubbed Winchester disks. Today IBM calls them *fixed disks,* which sounds as though they had once been broken. Most of the industry prefers the more general term *hard disk.*

The first IBM PCs had only single-sided floppy disk drives and a storage capacity of 160K per disk. At the time that seemed reasonable; the Apple II offered only 140K per disk, and the Osborne 1's disks held only 96K. When double-sided drives were introduced, the PC's disk capacity jumped to 320K (with DOS 1.10); with DOS 2.00 or a later version, disks can store 360K each.

But as programs became larger and more powerful, and as PCs took over more and more tasks involving vast amounts of data, what had seemed reasonable became inadequate for many users. Enter the hard disk, standard on the XT and optional on the PC. The XT's hard disk stores 10 megabytes, the equivalent of roughly 30 floppies.

Hard Disk Software

Preparing a hard disk drive for use with your PC can be a very simple or a very complicated procedure. Whenever necessary, seek assistance from your dealer in installing the drive and configuring the special software (if your drive requires it). As mentioned previously, you generally should not use the hard disk with special software designed for DOS 1.00 or 1.10; these versions of DOS were not designed to support hard disks, and an ever-increasing number of programs require DOS 2.00 or a later version.

In terms of the disk operating system, hard disks are much like floppy disks. For example, a hard disk must be formatted before it can be used. Almost all of the standard DOS commands that manipulate data on floppy disks can also be used with hard disks. Some DOS commands, however, are not meaningful when used with a hard disk. DISKCOMP and DISKCOPY are two commonly used commands that will not work with hard disks. But you can use the COPY and COMP commands with both floppy and hard disk drives.

One command that must be used with extreme care is FORMAT (a point that can't be emphasized enough). The FORMAT command in DOS 2.00 will format (and thereby erase) an entire hard disk just as readily as it will prepare a floppy disk for use. If you use a hard disk, you may wish to build a warning message into the FORMAT command so you don't mistakenly erase the contents of your hard disk. An experienced DOS user should be able to help you make the change, which can be accomplished with a batch file (see Chapters 4 and 10).

Like floppy disk drives, hard disk drives are designated as a single letter followed by a colon. The XT's hard disk drive is designated as drive C; if a second hard disk is added, it becomes drive D. You can, however, use the ASSIGN command in DOS 2.00 to change the drive designations. Some programs are designed to store all data on drive B, for example, but you can instruct DOS to store data on drive C with the ASSIGN command. Or you can make a hard disk drive the default drive by typing **ASSIGN A = C**.

If you have a non-IBM hard disk that has its own installation software, you may be able to divide the disk into several simulated drives, called *volumes*, that have their own letters. Although this procedure helps to keep you from mistakenly formatting the whole disk, it is no longer necessary for file organization, because DOS 2.00 and later versions allow for a series of subdirectories (see Chapter 10).

The manner in which you prepare a hard disk depends on the brand you have. Unless special software is required by your brand of disk drive, just follow the procedures described below and detailed in the IBM DOS manual. Remember that your dealer should be able to help you initialize your disk if you run into difficulties.

The FDISK program   FDISK is a DOS utility that sets up areas called *partitions* on the hard disk. (This process is similar to creating volumes on a non-IBM hard disk.) Some hard disk manufacturers other than IBM supply another program that accomplishes the same task. With these drives, use the supplied program instead of FDISK. Unless your hard disk drive has already been initialized, you must execute the FDISK program (or an equivalent) before you can use the disk. The FDISK program is covered in depth in the IBM DOS manual.

Partitions allow you to use the hard disk with more than one operating system. Unless you are planning to use an operating system other than PC-DOS, however, it is best to allocate only a single partition, since you can always create additional partitions for the other operating systems as the need arises. (You would have to back up all your DOS files on floppy disks, create the new partitions—which erases all data on the disk—and then load the files from the floppies onto the newly partitioned hard disk.) A single partition for DOS will allow you to use the entire hard disk for DOS files.

A hard disk partition is either active or not active, and only one partition can be active at a time. The active partition contains the operating system that will be loaded when the PC is first powered up (in the XT and in any other system that can boot from a hard disk when no disk is in the floppy disk drive). You can, of course, load any operating system from the floppy disk drive, and that procedure is necessary with many non-IBM hard disks.

All the information on a hard disk is stored in a finite number of areas called *cylinders*. Each cylinder can store 32,768 (or 32K) bytes of information. The IBM 10-megabyte hard disk, for example, contains 305 cylinders. Each one is numbered, and the first one is always 000. When specifying a partition, you must specify on what cylinder you would like the partition to begin and end.

FDISK options   When you first invoke FDISK, one of three things can happen, depending on how many hard disks are attached to the system. If no hard disks are attached to the system, an error message will appear on the screen. If you get this message and a hard disk is attached to the system, the disk probably isn't connected properly. If one hard disk drive is connected, a four-option menu will be displayed. If two hard disk drives are connected, a five-option menu will appear.

For each command in the FDISK program, you can enter your selection from the menu, or you can press the <Enter> key, and FDISK will supply a default response, which is displayed on the screen enclosed in brackets. Be sure to refer to the DOS manual when you run the FDISK program, so that you don't inadvertently choose an inappropriate option.

The first option enables you to set aside a partition to be used by DOS. If the hard disk already has a DOS partition, the screen will display an error message. Otherwise, it will ask whether you want to use the entire disk for PC-DOS. If you don't want to, FDISK will prompt you for all the information required to create the partitions.

The second FDISK option available from the main menu enables you to change the active partition if you have more than one partition on your hard disk. When you select this option, the status (active or not active), the type (DOS or non-DOS), and the starting and ending cylinder numbers of each partition on the hard disk will be displayed on the screen. At this point, all you have to do is select which partition you want active.

The third FDISK option deletes the DOS partition as well as all data in that DOS partition. This option should be used with caution, or you may find yourself losing megabytes of valuable information. Fortunately, FDISK reminds you that this option destroys data. Be sure to make backup copies of any files you might want to keep before deleting the DOS partition. If you want to use the partition of another operating system after deleting the DOS partition, you should change that partition to the active partition before you delete the DOS partition.

The fourth FDISK option provides a means by which you can display status information about the partitions of a hard disk. The starting and ending cylinder numbers of each partition are displayed, as well as whether the partition is active or not active and DOS or non-DOS.

The fifth option is meaningful only if more than one hard disk is attached to the PC. It allows you to perform any of the first four options from the FDISK main menu on the second hard disk.

Formatting the DOS partition   Once you have created the DOS partition, you cannot start using it immediately. Like a floppy disk, a hard disk must be formatted before it can be used. Partitioning doesn't format a hard disk; it allocates areas on the disk that are to be formatted and used by various operating systems.

As in the case of a floppy disk, the FORMAT command is used to format the DOS partition. You will probably want to use both the /S and the /V optional parameters when you format the

DOS partition. These parameters work the same with a hard disk as a floppy disk: /S transfers the operating system to the DOS partition, and /V allows you to specify a volume label for the partition. (When used with the COPY or DISKCOPY command, however, /V means verify.) If you do not transfer the system to the hard disk, you will not be able to boot from the hard disk even if your hard disk would otherwise have that capability. If you do not use the /V option, you will not be able to give the DOS partition a volume label without reformatting it, which will destroy any data that you have stored there.

When using the FORMAT command to format a hard disk partition, be sure to specify the drive letter (C or D) of the hard disk you want to format. Because a hard disk can store so much information, it takes much longer to format a hard disk than a floppy disk. Avoid keeping the FORMAT.COM file on the hard disk drive because, as mentioned previously, if the hard disk is the current drive and you want to format a floppy disk, it is far too easy to enter the FORMAT command without a drive designator. If this unfortunate event should occur, the DOS partition will be reformatted, and all data stored there will be lost.

Hard Disk Backup

The necessity of backing up a hard disk cannot be stressed enough. If something catastrophic happens to a standard floppy disk, you may lose up to 360K of priceless, irreplaceable data; with a hard disk, you can lose 5, 10, or more megabytes. Good computing procedure dictates that any file of any value whatsoever be backed up at least once on another disk.

Backing up a hard disk is usually much more complex than backing up a floppy disk. It is good practice to make at least one backup of your hard disk every day, although you need only back up the files that have changed since the last time the disk was backed up.

There isn't one standard, straightforward procedure for backing up a hard disk. A plethora of hard disk backup devices are available from a variety of manufacturers. Of course, a hard disk backup device is already built into your PC or XT—the floppy disk drive. The floppy disk drive is not an ideal backup device for a hard disk, however, because about 14 floppy disks are needed to back up a 5-megabyte hard disk. But floppy disks provide the most economical, although time-consuming, method of backing up a hard disk.

Removable hard disk cartridges Removable hard disk cartridges provide an almost ideal medium for making backups of hard disks. You can use the cartridge hard disk drive as your only hard disk drive and make backups by swapping cartridges in much the same way as you make backups of a floppy disk on a PC that has only one floppy disk drive. You can also use the cartridge drive as a backup device for a higher capacity hard disk drive. One disadvantage of a cartridge drive, like most other backup devices, is that it is considerably more expensive than backing up on floppy disks. Cartridge hard disk drives are competitively priced with fixed drives, however, and the expense should not be much of a factor if you want to use a cartridge drive instead of a fixed drive. To back up higher capacity hard disk drives, several cartridges may be required to back up all the data.

Magnetic tape storage   A number of manufacturers offer magnetic tape drives as backup devices for hard disks. Some externally mounted hard disk units (non-IBM) come with a tape drive in addition to the hard disk drive itself. Although tape backup is slower than backup on removable cartridges, it can be far more convenient than backup on floppy disks. And tape drives often have a greater storage capacity than hard disk cartridges, so in some ways tape is a better storage medium for backing up the higher capacity hard disk drives.

Several types of magnetic tape drives are available for backing up the hard disks used with the PC and the XT. A number of them accept tape cartridges. These devices are similar to cassette tape recorders, but they have been designed to store large amounts of digital information. A number of tape cartridges, such as standard video cassettes or ¼-inch tape cartridges, are used with these drives. Reel-to-reel tape drives are also available as hard disk backup devices. Because ½-inch reel-to-reel tape is a popular storage medium for large mainframe computers, you can exchange information with large computer systems using some of these reel-to-reel tape drives. (Such large-capacity tape systems can be more expensive than the hard disk, however.)

High-capacity floppy disk drives   Although the PC's floppy disk drives are not ideal for hard disk backup, a number of higher capacity floppy drives are available for use with the PC, and they may offer a more satisfactory solution to the problem of hard disk backup. IBM floppy disk drives are 40-track disk drives; they are capable of reading and writing 40 tracks on each surface of a disk. Eighty-track disk drives can store twice as much information (about 720K with double-sided drives) as 40-track disk drives. The IBM floppy disk controller board can work with these 80-track disk drives, although special software is required to use them with DOS.

These high-capacity 5¼-inch disk drives can make hard disk backup on floppy disks twice as fast. Although these disk drives may not be as convenient as other backup devices, they are on the average much lower in price. In addition, as with cartridge hard disk drives, these high-capacity floppy disk drives, with proper software, are treated by DOS like any other disk drives and needn't be used solely for hard disk backup.

Eight-inch floppy disk drives are also available for the PC. These disk drives require a special controller board and software to operate with DOS. A double-sided, double-density, 8-inch disk drive can store more than 1 megabyte of information. One advantage of an 8-inch drive is that with proper software you can exchange information with other computers that store data on the same type of drive. Like the high-capacity 5¼-inch drives, an 8-inch floppy drive may be used like any other disk drive and can also serve as a convenient means for hard disk backup.

Backup on standard floppy disks   Although numerous hard disk backup devices are available for the PC, it is feasible, if not particularly enjoyable, to back up your files on standard floppy disks. You need not back up the entire contents of the hard disk every day, and there are a number of ways to go about backing up. You can, for instance, make a complete backup on a certain date and at the end of each day make backup copies of all files that have been changed since that date or since the last complete backup.

The hard disk may also have come with special software for making backup files on floppy disks. BACKUP and RESTORE are two programs supplied with DOS that facilitate making and accessing backup copies of your hard disk files on floppy disks. The BACKUP command copies files from a hard disk to floppy disks. The RESTORE command allows you to transfer files that have been stored with the BACKUP command back to a hard disk.

BACKUP command   As with many other DOS commands, a number of required and optional parameters are used with the BACKUP command. The first parameter specifies the hard disk file or files that you would like to back up. This parameter consists of a hard disk drive designator (C or D) or the name of a file optionally preceded by a drive designator. The second parameter is the letter (A or B) of the floppy disk drive on which the backup copy will be recorded. If only a hard disk drive letter is specified as the first parameter, all files in the current directory, but not in the subdirectories of the current directory (unless you have specified the /S parameter discussed below), will be stored on the floppy disk. (See "DOS Commands and Tree-Structured Directories" in Chapter 10 for a discussion of subdirectories.) You may use the global file name characters (? and *) in a file specification in the first parameter.

You must use formatted floppy disks with the BACKUP command. The files copied onto floppy disks from a hard disk can be accessed through the RESTORE command only. The BACKUP command allows you to back up hard disk files (and groups of files) that are larger than the capacity of a single floppy disk; in this case, you will be instructed to insert another disk when one is full. You should label the disks according to the number (beginning with 01) that the BACKUP program displays whenever you are asked to insert a new disk. A disk cannot be used for both standard DOS files and hard disk backup files (those copied with the BACKUP command). If you insert a regular DOS disk (as opposed to a hard disk backup disk) when executing the BACKUP command, all preexisting data on that disk will be lost.

The /S parameter instructs BACKUP to store all files in subdirectories of the current directory (as well as files in the subdirectories of the subdirectories) in addition to all the files in the current directory. Unless you specify this parameter, none of the files in the subdirectories of the current directory will be backed up with the BACKUP command.

The /M parameter is very useful for backing up data; it allows you to back up only those files that have been modified since the last time the hard disk was backed up. This parameter is particularly convenient because some files (such as DOS command files and most commercial programs) are never modified.

The /A parameter instructs DOS to back up the hard disk files onto a disk that already contains files that have been backed up from the hard disk. The backup disk should already be in the drive when you specify this parameter. If you omit this parameter, any existing data on the backup disk will be lost.

The /D parameter allows you to back up those files that have been created or modified on or after a specified date. The format for the date is the same as with the DATE command in DOS. The general format of this parameter is /D:mm-dd-yy, where *mm* is a two-digit number representing the month, *dd* is a two-digit number representing the day of the month, and *yy* is a two-digit number representing the year.

The following are a few examples of the BACKUP command:

    BACKUP C:*.* A: /S
    BACKUP D: B: /D:9-24-84
    BACKUP C:\MYDIR\MYFILE.TXT A: /M /A

RESTORE command   The RESTORE command allows you to recover files that have been backed up with the BACKUP command. The first parameter is the drive designator (A or B) of the floppy disk drive that contains the backup disk. The second parameter is the specification for the file or files that you would like restored. These first two parameters are essentially the same as the first two parameters required by the BACKUP command, but they are reversed. As with the BACKUP command, global file name characters are acceptable in the hard disk file specification (the second parameter, in this case). If you are not using subdirectories (see Chapter 10) or you do not specify a path in the second parameter, the files will be restored to the current directory. You may have all backed up files restored to the current directory by omitting the name of a file in the second parameter.

The /S parameter is analogous to its counterpart used with the BACKUP command. This parameter allows you to restore the files backed up from subdirectories (files copied with a BACKUP command with the /S parameter). All files in subdirectories of the subdirectories of the specified directory (or current directory if no directory was specified) will also be restored.

The /P parameter enables you to restore files back to the hard disk selectively. When you include the /P parameter, the RESTORE command will not automatically restore read-only files (IBMBIO-.COM and IBMDOS.COM are hidden, read-only files) and those that have been changed since the last time they were backed up. You will be prompted to verify that you want these files restored.

The following are two examples of the RESTORE command:

RESTORE A: \MYDIR\MYFILE.TXT
RESTORE B: C:*.* /S /P

Practical Considerations for Hard Disk Users

Making backup copies of hard disk files may at first be a nuisance. Once you get into the habit of making backups frequently, however, the apparent hassle becomes just another standard operating procedure. Unless the hard disk is completely filled with useless data, you should get into the habit of making frequent backups. Don't get into the habit of making backups intermittently. Set aside a time each day (or whatever interval you think practical) to back up the hard disk. How frequently you do this depends on how many hours a day you use the PC or the XT and how many changes are typically made to the files on the hard disk. It is fairly easy to copy the files that you have just worked on to a floppy disk at the end of each work session.

A hard disk can store a huge amount of data acquired over months or even years. Although hard disks are generally very reliable, if anything should go wrong, all the data may be destroyed and lost forever in a matter of seconds. Although losing (inadvertently or otherwise) all the data on a floppy disk can mean hundreds of thousands of bytes, losing information on a hard disk can mean millions of bytes. Even if you could recreate all the information lost in a hard disk mishap, the process would be prohibitively expensive. So don't take any chances with your data: make backups regularly and frequently.

Applications programs with a hard disk   There is no question that hard disk drives increase the capability and usefulness of personal computers. Many applications in fact require the increased speed and storage capacity of the rigid medium. Unfortunately, however, a number of applications programs are designed primarily for floppy-disk-based systems. These programs may not allow you to take full or even partial advantage of a hard disk. In fact, some programs currently on the market do not even run with DOS 2.00.

Protected software invariably creates problems. You cannot generally transfer a protected program from a floppy disk to a hard disk. Even worse, some protected programs do not even allow you to save your data files on the hard disk. For programs like these, you can usually use the ASSIGN command in DOS to trick the applications program into believing that the hard disk is actually a floppy disk (drive B, generally).

Fortunately, for most common applications such as word processing and spreadsheet analysis, you can choose among a multitude of protected and unprotected packages. Yet some of the more innovative software is available in protected versions only. It is generally advisable to purchase unprotected programs even if you do not have a hard disk, because every program and data file of any value should be backed up.

Some protected programs allow limited use of a hard disk. You remove the protected disk as soon as the program has loaded, and carry out all operations using the hard disk. Some unprotected programs may not work with hard disks. Before you purchase any software, be sure to inquire whether the program will allow you to take advantage of a hard disk drive.

Tree-structured directories   The massive storage capacity of a hard disk drive enables you to store thousands of files on a single piece of magnetic medium. Although this capability frees you from the floppy disk shuffle and opens up previously impractical applications for your personal computer, keeping track of all those files can become a nightmare unless you take advantage of the tree-structured directory facilities of DOS (2.00 or later versions). A detailed discussion of tree-structured directories and batch files appears in Chapter 10; the following considerations are especially relevant to using hard disks.

You will find that files generally fall logically into groups. But organizing the files into logical groups on a hard disk requires a little planning. For example, you might want to keep all your word processing text files in a single directory or, if you have quite a few text files, in subdirectories (grouped by topic) of a single directory. Some applications programs, unfortunately, cannot use files in directories other than the current one. Any applications program designed to work with a hard disk should accommodate such files, however.

Batch files can simplify using an applications program with tree- structured directories. For example, you can have a batch file change directories (using the CD command), execute an applications program, and change back to the root directory when you have finished using the program. You might want to have such a batch file for each applications program you use with the hard disk. Using these batch files, you needn't keep track of which files are in which directory; the computer will keep track of that for you.

Tree-structured directories provide a convenient way to organize files in a logical, consistent manner. On a hard disk it is impractical to keep all files in a single directory. The tree-structured directory facilities of DOS aren't difficult to master, but take some time to become familiar with them. Although the single root directory may suffice for floppy disks, a more elaborate hierarchical directory structure is necessary for a hard disk. Once you have established a logical tree structure for your hard disk, you will be able to keep track of all your files.

Advanced Features of DOS

By now you should be feeling fairly comfortable with PC-DOS. Chapter 3 explained most of the DOS commands you will need to run your PC, and Chapters 2 and 4 presented others. But DOS offers many more capabilities that we haven't covered yet. If you have a PC, you won't need these commands, but learning them will give you more power when you are using your computer. If you are using an XT, you will need to use some of these DOS features, but you will probably want to use most of the others as well.

DOS Commands and Tree-Structured Directories
Computer terminology is rarely self-explanatory. For example, you might assume that the phrase *tree-structured directories* refers to directories that consist of files with names like REDWOOD, PINE, OAK, and WILLOW. Actually, the tree-structured directory facilities of DOS provide a convenient way to organize a large number of files. When a floppy disk is formatted, a single directory, called the *root directory,* is automatically created. The root directory is represented by a backslash. The root directory of a floppy disk can hold a maximum of either 64 or 112 files, depending upon whether the disk drive is single- or double-sided. Unless you tell the computer otherwise, all the files you use and create will be in the root directory.

 If you are using floppy disks, you may find it practical to keep one or more groups of related files in the root directory of a single

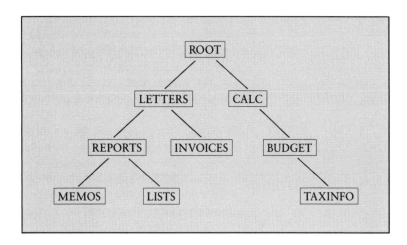

Figure 10.1 *Sample of tree-structured directories.*

disk. But if you use a hard disk, you will find it impractical to keep all your files in a single directory. Hard disk users will find tree-structured directories especially useful.

Creating a tree-structured directory is relatively simple. All directories other than the root directory are called subdirectories. Unlike the root directory, subdirectories are not limited in length, so you may have as many files in a subdirectory as disk space allows. You may also have as many subdirectories on a disk as space allows.

The names of subdirectories have the same format as the names of files: up to eight characters followed by a period and an extension of up to three characters. Although subdirectories are files, they cannot be used with the standard file manipulation commands, such as COPY and ERASE.

Subdirectories may have subdirectories of their own. Each subdirectory is listed in its parent directory, the one immediately above it in the hierarchy (with the root directory at the top). The directory structure of a disk is like an inverted tree with the root directory at the top and the subdirectories branching off from it and other subdirectories. Figure 10.1 illustrates the concept of tree-structured directories.

The directory displayed on the screen when you enter the DIR command is called the *current directory*. The current directory may be the root directory or a subdirectory. If you have not created any subdirectories, the current directory will automatically be the root directory. Files present on a directory other than the current directory are not listed in the current directory and cannot be used until you instruct DOS to go to another directory.

To place a file in a subdirectory or use a file that is already in a subdirectory, you must specify the *path* to that file. To indicate the path, you type a command (for the operation you want to perform with the file) followed by a backslash and the names of the subdirectories that DOS must go through to find that file. To display the contents of the file README.NOW (shown in Figure 10.1) on the screen, for example, you would type

TYPE README.NOW \LETTERS\REPORTS\MEMOS <Enter>

DOS would follow the path through the LETTERS subdirectory, then through REPORTS, and into MEMOS to find README-.NOW, and then display that file on the screen.

If the first character of the path is a backslash, as in the example above, DOS assumes that its search must begin with the root directory. If a backslash is not the initial character in a path, DOS assumes that the first directory in the path is a subdirectory of the current directory (which need not be the root directory).

Several utilities in DOS 2.00 or later versions are designed for use with tree-structured directories. They include MKDIR, which creates a subdirectory; RMDIR, which removes a subdirectory; CHDIR, which allows you to change directories; TREE, which displays a listing of all directories on a disk; and PATH, which designates a route through subdirectories. (The PATH command has a specific use. It can access programs or batch files but cannot access data files.)

MKDIR   Subdirectories are created with the MKDIR command (abbreviated MD). The general form of this command consists of MD (or MKDIR) followed by the name of the new directory and, optionally, a disk drive designator, a path specification, or both. For example, you might want to store all your spreadsheet files in a single directory. You can create such a directory by typing **MD CALC** <Enter>. The subdirectory CALC will now be listed in the current directory with <DIR> next to its directory name. To produce a directory listing of CALC, type **DIR CALC** <Enter>. The only listings in the CALC subdirectory are the "parent" or "overhead" directories, indicated by one period where the name of the first directory would be and two periods where the name of the second directory would be (see Figure 10.2). DOS creates these entries to identify each subdirectory and its position in the tree structure; they do not affect your use of the directories or the files.

To create a subdirectory of CALC called BUDGET, use the MD command again and type **MD CALC\BUDGET** <Enter>. If you type **DIR CALC** <Enter> again, you will see BUDGET listed in the directory.

RMDIR   Although subdirectories are files, they cannot be erased with the ERASE or DEL commands. You must remove a subdirectory in the manner in which it was created. The RMDIR

```
A>DIR CALC

Volume in drive A has no label
Director of A: \ CALC

.                  <DIR>      1-01-80      12:12a
. .                <DIR>      1-01-80      12:12a
2 File(s)                    11264 bytes free

A> _
```

Figure 10.2 *The CALC sub-directory showing markers for the "parent" files.*

command (abbreviated RD) has the opposite function of the MD command; it removes directories.

There are some limitations to removing directories, however, which are designed to protect your data. A subdirectory must be empty of all files and subdirectories (excluding the parent files, '.' and '..') before it can be removed. And you cannot remove the root directory or the current directory. To remove the CALC subdirectory we've just created, you first have to remove the BUDGET subdirectory. Type

RD CALC\BUDGET <Enter>
RD CALC <Enter>

and both subdirectories will be removed. The first command (**RD CALC\BUDGET** <Enter>) indicates the path from the current directory (in this case, the root directory), through the CALC subdirectory, to the BUDGET subdirectory. Once BUDGET has been removed from CALC, CALC itself can be removed.

CHDIR   Using files in subdirectories becomes more convenient when a subdirectory is made the current directory with the CHDIR command (abbreviated CD). The format of this command is the same as that of the MD and RM commands. If you wish to change directories, type **CD** <Enter> followed by the path of the subdirectory.

A Sample Structure

To illustrate the use of a tree-structured directory, let's assume that you're working on a project in which you must analyze the productivity of three personal computer manufacturers. The project will involve using a word processing program to write reports and a spreadsheet program to analyze numerical data. Because a project such as this one will no doubt require many files, a series of subdirectories will be quite useful.

The first step in organizing the files is to create a subdirectory that will contain all files related to the project, which you can do by typing **MD \PCPROJCT** <Enter>. The three microcomputer manufacturers you will study are IBM, Apple, and Eagle. You can create a separate subdirectory for each company by typing the following lines. (As always, press <Enter> after each line.)

MD \PCPROJCT\IBM

MD \PCPROJCT\APPLE

MD \PCPROJCT\EAGLE

You might want to create separate subdirectories in each of these subdirectories for spreadsheets and reports. For the IBM directory, you would type

MD \PCPROJCT\IBM\CALC

MD \PCPROJCT\IBM\REPORT

Then you would create analogous subdirectories for the Apple and Eagle subdirectories. Your completed directory structure should resemble the one shown in Figure 10.3.

Once you've created a directory structure, you can store files in the appropriate directories. The simplest way is to use the CD (change directories) command to make the desired subdirectory the current directory. Any files you create will automatically be placed there without having to enter additional commands. To do this, you probably would have to have a copy of the applications program you will use in that same directory, because most PC software (including most spreadsheet and word processing programs) is not compatible with the subdirectory system. You can't create a file with one of these programs and specify that it be located in a directory other than the current one.

One alternative is to use the applications program the usual way, creating all files in the root directory where the programs would logically be located, and copying the files to their appropriate subdirectories later. This is a relatively simple process. You can also copy any of your present files to subdirectories as long as the subdirectory system has been created. For example, if you wanted to copy worksheet files about IBM into the proper subdirectory, you would type

COPY IBM*.WKS \PCPROJCT\IBM\CALC <Enter>

if your worksheet files about IBM all began with IBM and ended with the extension .WKS. After verifying that the files have been copied into the CALC subdirectory, you can erase those files from their original directory.

This procedure of copying files to subdirectories may be the most practical one for use with applications programs, because you would needlessly use up disk space by storing a copy of the applica-

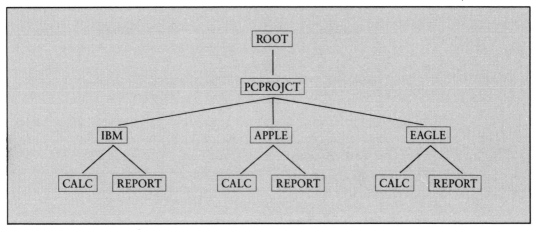

Figure 10.3 *Tree-structured directories for the computer research project.*

tions program in each subdirectory where you want to store files created with the program.

By organizing your files in a system of subdirectories, you may never have to worry about keeping track of them. But if you do get lost in such an elaborate structure, DOS has a utility that displays the directory and the file structure. The TREE command displays the tree structure of a specified disk on the screen. All the directory paths on that disk are displayed. If you add a /F parameter at the end of the command, all the file names will also be displayed. You can also include a disk drive designator as a parameter with the TREE command. Two examples of the proper format of the tree command are **TREE** <Enter> and **TREE B**: **/F** <Enter>. Figure 10.4 shows the response to the TREE command for the disk containing the directories for the sample computer research project involving IBM, Apple, and Eagle.

The PATH command allows you to use programs and batch files in directories other than the current directory. To locate a program or a batch file (but not a data file), you can specify a path through one or more subdirectories by using a command such as **PATH \LETTERS\REPORTS** <Enter>. If a program is located in either the LETTERS or the REPORTS subdirectory, DOS will look there for it. You would have to type only the program's name; DOS would then locate it and initiate the program. To use the program CATA-LOG.COM stored in the REPORTS subdirectory, you would type

PATH\LETTERS\REPORTS <Enter>

CATALOG <Enter>

Now that you have seen how to climb through the hierarchies of tree-structured directories, you are ready to organize all the files on your disks. Although you may not need to use this directory sys-

```
DIRECTORY PATH LISTING FOR VOLUME ??????????

Path:    \PCPROJCT
Sub-directories:     IBM
                     APPLE
                     EAGLE


Path:    \PCPROJCT\IBM
Sub-directories:     CALC
                     REPORT


Path:    \PCPROJCT\IBM\CALC
Sub-directories:     None


Path:    \PCPROJCT\IBM\REPORT
Sub-directories:     None


Path:    \PCPROJCT\APPLE
Sub-directories:     CALC
                     REPORT


Path:    \PCPROJCT\APPLE\CALC
Sub-directories:     None


Path:    \PCPROJCT\APPLE\REPORT
Sub-directories:     None


Path:    \PCPROJCT\EAGLE
Sub-directories:     CALC
                     REPORT


Path:    \PCPROJCT\EAGLE\CALC
Sub-directories:     None


Path:    \PCPROJCT\EAGLE\REPORT
Sub-directories:     None
```

Figure 10.4 *Response to the TREE command showing directory organization for the computer research project.*

tem when you first use the PC (you can stay with the root directory indefinitely), you may find the system useful as you accumulate a large number of files and projects. If you are using an XT or a PC with a hard disk, however, you'll probably find that a tree-structured directory is necessary, or at least highly useful.

Batch Commands

In Chapter 4 you learned to write some simple batch files. Let's review batch files and then explore other ways to put them to use. Batch files are much like recipes, although they don't consist of instructions for preparing a batch of some gourmet concoction; they contain instructions for preparing a plate of DOS commands. Batch commands enable you to execute a number of DOS instructions simultaneously. Rather than typing in the same group of commands each time you want to perform a certain DOS operation, you type in only the name of a batch file. Batch commands not only save a great deal of time, they also significantly reduce the likelihood of operator errors.

Any DOS command can be used in a batch file. A batch file contains one or more DOS instructions and always has the file name extension .BAT. To execute the commands contained in a batch file, just type in the batch file name (you can omit the .BAT extension when executing a batch file). You may create a batch file using the COPY command or use a text editor such as EDLIN.

AUTOEXEC.BAT is a special batch file that, if present, executes automatically when you turn on the system or reboot. It is just like any other batch file, however, in that it may be executed from DOS at any other time by typing AUTOEXEC. Many software packages include AUTOEXEC.BAT files to assist the user in running the application. However, occasionally you may want to halt the execution of an AUTOEXEC.BAT or some other batch file. As with all DOS operations, you can usually stop the execution of a batch file by pressing <Ctrl>-<Break>. If you press <Ctrl>-<Break> and other commands are still in the batch file that have not yet been executed, the current operation will be aborted and the message 'Terminate batch job (Y/N)?_' displayed. You must decide whether to abort the batch instructions entirely or continue with the remaining operations.

Using and experimenting with batch files is the best way to discover all the ways you can take advantage of them. For example, occasionally you might want to make copies of all the BASIC programs on a given floppy disk. Such a precaution might prove useful in the event that a program is inadvertently erased or the disk develops a defective sector. The command **COPY *.BAS *.BA2** <Enter> will perform this task for you. Rather than typing in this rather cumbersome command each time you want to make copies of your BASIC programs, with a single batch file you can type it in only once. Using the COPY command, you can readily create a batch file to accomplish this task. Type

COPY CON DUPLIC.BAT <Enter>
COPY *.BAS *.BA2 <F6> <Enter>

To execute this batch file, type **DUPLIC** <Enter> from the A prompt. After typing DUPLIC, note that the command appears on the screen as if you had typed it in yourself.

Another useful batch file can display a wide directory and a disk status report. Type the following commands, pressing <Enter> after each line:

```
COPY CON DIRCHK.BAT
DIR /W
CHKDSK <F6>
```

Type **DIRCHK** <Enter> to execute this batch file.

One of the most useful batch files is an AUTOEXEC.BAT file that initiates the use of a program. For example, to display the date and time and load *WordStar* automatically, type

```
COPY CON AUTOEXEC.BAT
DATE
TIME
WS <F6>
```

Note that you must use the DATE and TIME commands in the batch file in order to have DOS prompt you for the correct time and date when you are using an AUTOEXEC.BAT file.

Replaceable parameters   Many DOS commands are used with mandatory or optional parameters. These parameters are generally used to indicate disk drive designators or the names of files. Because the parameters will probably be different each time a batch file is executed, in creating the batch file you will need to specify dummy parameters to represent the actual parameters. The actual parameters will be placed where the dummy parameters are specified when the batch file is executed. Dummy parameters are indicated by the percent sign preceding any single-digit number (%0, %1, %2, and so on). The %0 symbols denote the name of the batch file itself, %1 the first parameter, %2 the second parameter, and so forth.

Replaceable parameters make batch commands far more useful. For example, in the DIRCHK.BAT file above, there was no way to designate a certain disk drive or a specific file. But we can with replaceable parameters. Type

```
COPY CON DIRCHK.BAT
DIR %1 /W
CHKDSK %1 <F6>
```

This batch file is functionally identical to the one above it when no parameter is specified. But now you can execute either DIRCHK B: or DIRCHK MYFILE. Typing **DIRCHK B:** <Enter> asks for a directory of all files on drive B; typing **DIRCHK MYFILE** <Enter> asks for a directory of all files with the name MYFILE.

Three subcommands make batch file operations considerably more useful by providing a way for the computer to communicate with you during batch file execution. By making liberal use of these subcommands, you need not be concerned with what the computer is doing while a batch file is executing.

ECHO subcommand   The ECHO subcommand can stop and start the automatic display of DOS commands as they are being executed from a batch file. This subcommand may also be used to display messages while a batch file is in the process of executing. You may want to suspend the automatic display of DOS commands as they are executed so that the screen will not be cluttered or so that an inexperienced user will not be confused by strange-looking DOS commands.

To disable the automatic display of commands, place an ECHO OFF command at the beginning of the batch file. Note that the ECHO OFF command is displayed as it is executed, although the commands following it are not. You can determine whether ECHO is on or off at any time from DOS simply by typing **ECHO** <**Enter**>. Normally ECHO is on.

It is often useful to display a message during the execution of a batch file. To do this, put an ECHO command in the batch file followed by the message on the same line. Let's use the ECHO command in the DIRCHK example. Type

COPY CON DIRCHK.BAT
ECHO OFF
ECHO   ** DIRECTORY AND STATUS REPORT ******
DIR %1 /W
CHKDSK %1
ECHO ON <**F6**>

At times, you may want to include remarks in a batch file. Although you can display comments with the ECHO subcommand, you may want to include general comments regarding the purpose of the batch file by using the REM subcommand. The REM subcommand consists of the word *REM* followed by a comment on the same line. Remarks can be up to 123 characters long. Unless the ECHO feature is turned off, the remarks (along with the word REM) will be displayed on the screen while the batch file is being executed. Let's put some remarks in a batch file:

COPY CON REMARK.BAT
REM   This is a sample batch file that demonstrates the REM command.
REM   These REMarks will be displayed when this batch file is executed.
ECHO OFF
REM   This remark will not be displayed.
ECHO ON <**F6**>

PAUSE subcommand The PAUSE subcommand provides yet another way to display a message. It halts the execution of a batch file and displays the message 'Strike a key when ready..._'. At this point, you must press any key to resume execution of the batch file. The PAUSE subcommand can be used to provide another variation of the DIRCHK batch file. Type the following:

```
COPY CON DIRCHK.BAT
ECHO OFF
ECHO        **** DIRECTORY AND STATUS REPORT ****
DIR %1 /W
ECHO   Status report coming up
PAUSE
CHKDSK %1
ECHO ON <F6>
```

When you run the batch file, two messages will be displayed below the directory listing: the 'Status report coming up' that you typed, and the PAUSE subcommand's 'Strike a key when ready...'.

IF subcommand Occasionally, you might want to have a batch file perform certain operations only if specified conditions are met. Conditional execution of DOS commands in a batch file is accomplished by using the IF subcommand. You may want to have a batch file that performs different functions, depending upon the value of a replaceable parameter. Let's construct a batch file that will display the directory entry of a file specified by the first parameter (%1) no matter what the second parameter is. And if an optional second parameter (%2) has the value of *T*, the contents of the designated file (%1) will also be displayed on screen. Type the following:

```
COPY CON DIRTYP.BAT
DIR %1
IF %2 = = T TYPE %1 <F6>
```

In this example, if you wish to have the computer type out the contents of the file in addition to its directory entry, you must enter a second parameter of *T*. If you do not specify a second parameter, an innocuous syntax error message will be displayed. To display the directory entry and the contents of MYFILE.TXT, type

```
DIRTYP MYFILE.TXT T <Enter>
```

As you have probably noticed, there are a quite a few similarities between batch subcommands and BASIC programming commands. But the syntax often differs. In BASIC, for example, one equal sign suffices in an IF statement, but two are required in a batch file.

In many instances, you may need to determine whether a file exists before performing certain DOS operations, just as a baker must determine whether all the ingredients are available before starting to make a cake. The computer can execute a particular command in a batch IF command on the condition that a specified file exists. For example, let's create a batch file that will display a directory of a specified file name if such a file exists. Type the following example:

```
COPY CON MAKEFILE.BAT
ECHO OFF
ECHO This file helps prevent duplication of file names.
IF EXIST %1 DIR %1 <F6>
```

The IF subcommand dramatically increases the usefulness of batch files. You can also negate the condition in an IF command by placing the word *NOT* immediately after the word *IF*. In the batch file just created you might want to include the command

```
IF NOT EXIST %1 ECHO File %1 does not exist
```

This command will check the disk's contents to see if the named file already exists, and will answer with a message on the screen.

Because any DOS command can be executed in a batch file, you can have your computer perform a series of complex operations while you sit back and watch. You can easily create recipes that have DOS commands as the ingredients. You needn't be an experienced programmer to start cooking up batch files, just as you needn't be a master chef to make dinner.

Other Useful DOS Commands

Three additional commands can be useful for working with DOS.

BREAK Despite its name, this command will not destroy anything in the PC. The BREAK command allows you to terminate a program by pressing <Ctrl>-<Break> simultaneously whenever DOS is carrying out any function for that program. DOS checks to see whether <Ctrl>-<Break> has been entered from the keyboard only when screen, keyboard, printer, or asynchronous operations are in progress. When a program is doing some other operation, the BREAK signal will not interrupt it. This limitation to the BREAK signal is called BREAK OFF.

You can turn BREAK on, however, and then DOS will check for <Ctrl>-<Break> whenever it performs any operations for a program. (But even with BREAK on, you may still be unable to terminate programs that do not make use of DOS function calls.)

The BREAK feature is usually off when DOS is first loaded. You can turn this feature on by typing **BREAK ON** <Enter> and turn it off by typing **BREAK OFF** <Enter>. Typing **BREAK** <Enter> by itself produces a message that indicates whether the BREAK feature is on or off.

PROMPT   The PROMPT command may not get you to work on time, but it can relieve you of the monotony of that ever-present DOS prompt, the greater-than sign (>) preceded by the designator of the current disk drive. This command allows you to replace the standard prompt with any other symbol or combination of characters that you want. The format of the PROMPT command consists of the word *PROMPT* followed by a string of text. If you want a personalized prompt, you can type **PROMPT JANE** <**Enter**> when Jane is using the computer. In this case, the characters will be displayed as you have typed them, so if you want Jane with only a capital *J,* type **PROMPT Jane** <**Enter**>.

Although you may only want to change the prompt to something more appropriate—such as "Your wish is my command"—by using special combinations of characters, you can have the prompt display a great deal of useful information. These special combinations, called *metastrings,* consist of two characters each: a dollar sign followed by one of a set of specific characters. Each of these characters represents either a certain symbol that otherwise cannot be entered in the text of a PROMPT command or a special kind of DOS information.

If you wanted to change the prompt to a dollar sign (one of the metastring symbols), you would type **PROMPT $$** <**Enter**>, and the prompt would change to the dollar sign. Other useful prompt changes include PROMPT $t, which displays the time from the computer's clock; PROMPT $d, which displays the date entered when DOS was loaded; and PROMPT A$g, which returns the original A prompt.

If you use the time or date prompt, you must enter the correct date and time when you turn on the computer, or use a special utility program and a battery-operated clock (a common option with add-on memory boards for the PC). If you neglect to enter the date or the time and are not using an automatic clock, you'll get the familiar 'Tue 1-01-80' greeting as the prompt for the date, and the actual number of seconds since you entered DOS as the time (displayed in the form '0:00:32.5').

VER   The VER command is used to display the version number of DOS that you are using. DOS version numbers are expressed as a major revision number followed by a decimal point and a two-digit minor revision number. The VER command is only available in DOS 2.00 or later versions. To determine the version of the DOS that you are using, type **VER** <**Enter**>, and the screen will display the version number.

You now have a better idea of what DOS can do. Although these additional features may be more than you will ever need, don't let the vast capabilities of this operating system overwhelm you. Rather than trying to digest them all in one sitting, take one at a time. The next time you need one of these features or simply have a free hour or two, dig out this chapter and add a new DOS feature to your repertoire.

CHAPTER ELEVEN

Caring for Your Equipment

Unlike automobiles, computers don't develop oil leaks or flat tires. A program may "crash," but nothing bends or breaks when that happens. The "engine" of your PC is made up of solid-state electronic components that don't move or wear out. Nevertheless, inadequate care of your computer, like poor automobile maintenance, can leave you stranded down the road.

While the modular construction of the PC makes repair relatively simple, it is not a job for the amateur. Unless you have an expensive service contract that provides on-site service, obtaining repair service means the inconvenience of having to take your PC to the shop, and, even worse, having to part with it for a few days. Since many breakdowns are avoidable, prevention is the best route.

Dirt, Dust, and Smoke

One of the major causes of computer failure is environmental contamination. Although a personal computer has few moving parts, those few parts are sensitive to airborne dirt, dust, and smoke particles. These contaminants can interfere directly with the disk drives and the keyboard. A buildup of dust on electronic components acts as a blanket, retaining heat and possibly precipitating early breakdown.

The most effective prevention, of course, is to keep dust out of the computer's environment. Locate your PC system in as dust-free an area as possible, and clean the room frequently. Although limited vacuuming near the computer is helpful, avoid using any appliance that has an electric motor near the PC or the XT. Such proximity can cause static electricity that may disrupt the computer's normal operation.

Mainframe computers are kept in carefully controlled environments. Although this is not necessary for PCs, a bit of attention to the environment can save a lot of bytes. It's a good idea to avoid eating or smoking in the computer room. Drinking is no problem if the liquid stays in the cup, but if it doesn't, serious damage can result. If you do drink in the computer room, place your cup where spills would not reach the computer, the printer, or the disks.

When your PC or XT is not in use, it is a good idea to keep the system covered. A number of companies manufacture cloth or vinyl dust covers for the PC. Separate covers are available for the system unit, the monitor, the keyboard, and the printer. Smaller plastic covers are available for the components most susceptible to damage: the keyboard and the disk drives. Although these covers won't protect the entire system, they are more convenient than full covers.

Another environmental hazard is static electricity. If you have ever gotten a shock when reaching for a doorknob after walking across a carpeted room or have felt a tingling sensation removing a long-sleeved polyester shirt, you have experienced static electricity. It can also be present without your being aware of it—anytime two materials come into contact and then separate. A rubbing action such as the two examples above or simply shifting in your chair intensifies static buildup.

Computer chips and data stored on floppy disks are extremely sensitive to static. A single "zap" too minute for you to detect can jumble data or damage a chip. Static isn't usually a problem in areas of high humidity, but as the humidity drops the static level tends to increase sharply. And because heaters dry out the air, static is a problem during the winter months. Air conditioners also have a dehumidifying effect, so if you use one, you can even run into static problems during the summer.

You can reduce or eliminate static electricity by using an antistatic chair mat, which drains away any static charges before they have a chance to build up, or by using an antistatic spray. Although the spray requires periodic reapplication, it has the advantage of controlling static sources throughout the room, not just under your chair. For areas that shouldn't be sprayed, such as the computer itself, disposable towelettes saturated with staticide are available.

Increasing the humidity of your computer room will lessen the likelihood of static damage. While having a humidifier in the room is the obvious way to do this, a more decorative solution may be an uncovered tropical fish tank.

PC Power

People need food to function. Give them too much, too little, or the wrong kind, and problems arise. The same is true for computers. Their food, however, is neither éclairs nor eggplant, but electricity. Most personal computers can cope with variations in line voltage of about 10 percent from the normal 120 volts. Your PC or XT, however, should be able to handle somewhat greater variations, but too much fluctuation in power can damage your data, your computer, or both.

Overvoltage (known as spikes or transients if extremely brief, and surges if slightly longer), can overload the CPU's circuits and damage its components. Undervoltage includes brownouts, shorter dips or sags, and complete power failures or blackouts.

Undervoltage, or power failure, instantly wipes out the computer's memory; whatever has been in RAM won't be. Anything you have saved on disk, however, will remain intact. But if you are in the process of reading from or writing to a disk at the moment of power loss, some of the disk sectors being accessed could be damaged. Keeping current backup copies of all your work will help prevent such a crisis.

Even in the unlikely event that at the exact instant the power fails or dips you happen to be updating your backup, your data should still be all right because both the DISKCOPY and COPY commands use only one disk drive at a time. Information is read from the source disk into memory, then the information in memory is written to the target disk. For extremely critical data, you can eliminate even the slightest chance of a total loss by using three disks in a rotating backup system. Even if something unforeseen happens to the PC while both the original and a backup are in it, you'll still have the second backup.

If you are in an area that has frequent power outages or reductions, you might want to add an uninterrupted power supply (UPS) to your system. A UPS consists of a heavy-duty rechargeable storage battery, a converter, and a device that instantly switches to the backup system at the slightest sign of trouble. Most commercial UPS systems cost between $400 and $800.

Although undervoltage itself won't damage the system's hardware, what goes down will eventually come back up; resumption of normal power is often accompanied by momentary overvoltage. You won't have time to react to a dip or a sag in power, but in the event of a blackout turn off your system and wait until several minutes after power resumes before turning it back on.

In addition to fluctuations in the power delivered to your building, appliances in your house can cause voltage variations. A refrigerator, an air conditioner, a vacuum cleaner, or even a coffee maker can draw enough power to wreak havoc. If possible, put the computer on its own circuit.

If power in your area tends to be uncertain, or if your PC shares its line with power-greedy appliances, consider putting a surge suppressor between the wall outlet and the computer's power cord. Surge suppressors contain circuits that dissipate the excess power of spikes and surges before it can reach the computer. Some include a fuse or a circuit breaker that shut down the computer if the overvoltage is so great that the surge suppressor can't correct it. They are available from most computer stores and typically cost between $60 and $100.

Do you need a surge suppressor? That's like asking if you need a roll bar or insurance for your car. You'll probably be all right without either, but caution is advisable.

So far we've examined the electrical equivalents of starving and overeating. But what about bad food? Electromagnetic interference (EMI) can make your wall outlet deliver electrical nourishment that suits your PC no better than last month's custard-filled éclairs would suit you.

EMI, or "noise," can be caused by distant lightning, nearby auto ignition noise, radio-frequency interference, and other natural and man-made factors. If you are in a residential neighborhood that has underground utilities, you might never have a problem. But if you are in an industrial area or one where the power lines have supported several generations of sparrows, your wall outlet probably isn't delivering the electrical equivalent of natural food.

Line noise will not damage your computer, but it can threaten the integrity of your data. Just as noise on the telephone lines can garble spoken information, line noise can garble electronic information. Noise filters, sometimes called power conditioners, are available either separately or combined with surge suppressors.

Shake and Bake

Even if they have clean air and clean electricity, computers have two potential enemies waiting in the wings—vibration and heat. Vibration, or motion, while deserving careful attention with portable computers, usually isn't much of a problem for the PC. The only thing that might cause vibration problems is the printer. Ideally, it should be on a separate table, isolated from the computer. Lacking this, place a pad or other shock-absorbing material under the printer to soak up vibrations. If your desk is at all wobbly, you may want to add bracing to stabilize it.

If you have to move the PC, be careful to avoid bumps and vibration. If you'll be moving the system any distance, repack it in the original boxes. If you have saved the cardboard inserts originally packed in the disk drives, put them in and close the drives' doors. Otherwise, put an old disk in each drive to lock the heads in place and protect them.

Many personal computers tend to overheat; when this happens, they may lose data from RAM. The PC, thankfully, is not on this list. IBM's reputation for building reliable products seems well deserved. The cooling fan in the PC is effective; in conjunction with well-placed ventilation openings, it assures a steady flow of air over the chips, the boards, and the disk drives.

Because a hard disk and its controller card generate more heat than a floppy, the XT has a more powerful fan than the PC and is thus protected from overheating. If you add a hard disk to a PC by buying the IBM Expansion Unit or some other external hard disk, you should have no problems. Be aware, however, that adding an internal hard disk to the PC system unit may cause difficulties. If you plan to install an internal hard disk, talk to a technician or consult other users to determine which manufacturers' disks have performed well.

As noted previously, dust is an insulator. A buildup of dust on electronic components can cause their temperature to rise, endangering both the components and the data they handle. By one estimate, a 25-degree increase in temperature equals a 50-percent decrease in component life—a good reason to keep your PC and its environment dust-free.

There is one more way in which heat can affect your PC. Every time you turn the computer on it warms up, and the rise in temperature causes components to expand. When you turn the computer off, the process is reversed—components contract. Thermal stress can eventually lead to component failure. While IBM expects you to turn the PC on and off, don't use the switch more than necessary. Some people leave their PCs on continuously, though that solution may seem extreme. A good compromise might be to turn the computer off when you're done for the day or will be gone for several hours, but leave it on when you're just going for coffee, a short meeting, or lunch.

One precaution you should take any time the computer is on but not in use is to turn down the brightness control on the monitor. Otherwise, after about ten minutes without change, whatever is displayed will begin to etch permanently into the screen.

Disk Care

The basics of caring for floppy disks are aptly summarized in the six rules printed on the back of the disk storage envelope supplied with most disks.

Protect the disk. Keep your disks in their protective envelopes except when you are using them.

Do not bend. "Floppy" means that the disk can flex—not that it should. Never bend or flex a disk.

Insert carefully. There are eight ways to put in a disk; only one is correct. The label should be face up, and the edge opposite the label should go in first. If the disk doesn't slide easily into the drive, remove it and try again; never force a disk into or out of a drive.

Do not touch. Hold the disk by the black protective sleeve—do not touch the disk surface itself.

50° F to 125° F. Don't expose the disks to excessive heat or cold, and don't leave them in direct sunlight. If you get an error message shortly after bringing a disk in from outside, allow the disk to adjust to room temperature, and try again. The slight change in size resulting from expansion or contraction may have caused the problem.

No magnets. Because the data is magnetically encoded on the disks, any magnetic charge can change or erase what is stored on them. So keep your disks away from magnets, including motors (such as tape recorders), telephones (whose ringing mechanism uses an electromagnet), and radio or stereo speakers. A distance of about a foot should be sufficient.

Since excessive pressure on a disk can destroy data, never use a pencil or a ball-point pen to write on a disk's label. Either use a felt-tip pen, or fill out the label before attaching it to the disk. Do not use an eraser on or near a disk, because the residue can contaminate the disk. Never put a paper clip on a disk; in addition to the pressure it exerts, paper clips tend to pick up a magnetic charge.

The boxes disks come in provide a safe home for them when they are not in use. If access to the disks is not as convenient as you might like, you can use a hinged plastic storage box that holds up to 50 disks.

Although the disks themselves should never been cleaned, you might want to clean the disk drives. Special cleaning disks are available that remove any buildup of iron oxide (the magnetic material that coats the disks) from the drives' read/write heads. This procedure is controversial, however. Some technicians claim that the abrasive surface of the cleaning disks can wear down the heads and cause more problems than they cure. Others insist that the cleaning disks do no harm and recommend using them every few months. A safe middle course would be to use a cleaning disk only if you are having problems. Don't subject your drives to regular cleaning, but if you are getting read/write errors (the computer displays an error message), such a cleaning might solve the problem.

The PC Connection

Even if you feed your PC good air, good electricity, and good disks, it's still possible that some day your computer may go on strike. But before you call out the National Guard, check for the most likely culprit: a loose connection. Is the power cord plugged into the wall outlet? Is power reaching the outlet? Make sure that you are not using an outlet that is controlled by a wall switch. Is the monitor's power cord plugged in?

Also check the system's cables. The little screws and clips that hold the cables in place may be a nuisance, but they serve a purpose. Make sure that they are secure. If checking doesn't solve the problem, unplug the computer, remove the cover, and check that all the plug-in boards are secure and that no chips have come loose. Even if you're not having trouble, it's a good idea to go through this routine occasionally, especially when you move your PC.

The IBM Diagnostics Disk

If the problem isn't a loose connection, you'll need to put the Diagnostics disk to work. In Chapter 2 you used some sections of this disk to learn about menu-driven programs. This time, start from the beginning and follow the menus. The "Problem Determination Procedures" section in the IBM *Guide to Operations* should provide additional assistance. As with any program, it's a good idea to make a copy of the Diagnostics distribution disk, then put the original away for safekeeping and work with the copy.

In Chapter 2 we stopped after the disk finished checking the various screen displays. If you continue with the Diagnostics, the program will present the information shown in Figure 11.1. 'XXX' will be either 400 or 500. A "scratch disk" is like a scratch pad: it is either blank, or whatever is on it is disposable. If you remove the Diagnostics disk (the necessary elements of its program have been loaded into RAM) and substitute a scratch disk, the computer

```
SYSTEM UNIT    XXX

****  WARNING  ****
DATA WILL BE DESTROYED

INSERT SCRATCH DISKETTE IN DRIVE A
PRESS ENTER WHEN READY
? _
```

Figure 11.1 *Warning displayed on the screen when checking disk drives with the Diagnostics program.*

will test drive A by writing on the disk, then reading what it wrote. If you have two drives, it will carry out the same procedure with drive B.

When a diagnostic test is successful, a number ending in two zeros (200, 300, and so on) is displayed. If the program finds a problem, it will display an error message along with a number not ending in zero. Jot down both the message and the number. This information will allow your dealer to pinpoint the difficulty.

An Advanced Diagnostics program is also available from IBM. While it is intended primarily for dealers and service technicians, it is included with the *IBM Hardware Maintenance and Service* manual, which sells for $150. That price may sound high, but if you're willing to dig inside your PC when something goes wrong, the manual and the program can save you many times that cost in repair bills. The Advanced Diagnostics disk works much like the standard Diagnostics disk but goes into more detail. If you have a disk drive problem, for example, it allows you to choose from four tests to isolate the source of the problem.

Insurance

The best insurance, of course, is prevention. But what if worse comes to worst and a fire or a theft suddenly leaves you without a computer? "No problem, I have insurance." Do you? If your PC is at home and you use it for business, you might be surprised to find that your homeowner's policy excludes the computer. Even if it is covered, is it covered for purchase price, current value, or replacement cost? It's best to find out before a catastrophe—not after. While you're going over your coverage with an insurance agent, ask about software. Some policies cover the replacement of lost or damaged programs. If your regular policy doesn't provide the coverage you want, contact one or more insurance agencies to determine if they offer special personal computer insurance and compare both costs and coverage.

Keep in mind that insurance policies don't cover the data you so painstakingly accumulate, though some allow for the cost of re-entering lost data. The best insurance is storing backup copies in a separate location.

Optimum Care

Caring for a computer is like caring for your health. Since the results of poor care usually don't show up immediately, it is easy to get into bad habits. On the other hand, it is also easy to become a hypochondriac. If you keep your PC in a sealed, air-conditioned room, cover every component before answering the phone, and make endless backups, you will probably avoid most problems. But you also may not get much work done.

A computer is a tool and should be treated accordingly. Aim for optimum care, not maximum care. After all, the only way to make sure that the PC never fails is to leave it packed in the box. Preventive maintenance seems to follow the 20-80 rule: 20 percent of the possible effort gives 80 percent protection. Do more, and your rate of return begins to diminish. The basic rule for computer care is use the tool but don't abuse it.

Tips for Troubleshooting

■ If a hardware component functions improperly or stops working, check all the unit's cables and connections. The cable or the cord often becomes slightly dislodged, thereby breaking the connection even though it appears to be intact.

■ Computers can be subject to intermittent errors, particularly in their memory components. If the PC or the XT displays a memory error message but is otherwise operating normally, quickly back up the work currently in progress, then turn off the machine for a few moments. When you turn the computer on again, the error message may not reappear. Check your data carefully; if no work has been lost, the error may have been an intermittent one, and you can continue to use the computer until the error recurs.

■ Whenever you see an error message on the screen, write down its exact wording before taking action. The computer or data will not be harmed if you wait a few moments. If possible, check the manual of the program you are using for an explanation of the error before rebooting or otherwise removing the message from the screen. The DOS manual and most other manuals document error messages and may suggest remedies for the problem.

■ Keep a record of error messages and equipment malfunctions, including the date and the circumstances under which the problem occurred. This practice is especially useful for intermittent errors; you may document a series of errors over time that can provide appropriate clues to an underlying problem. Always give a detailed account of the problem; these details could save time and money when a technician is trying to solve the problem.

Computer Ergonomics

Computers are remarkably error-free. Most of the errors blamed on them are really people's errors. Some errors occur at the programming stage; a program is designed in such a way that it is not flexible enough to deal with the variety of information that will be processed. Other errors occur at the data entry stage, usually in the form of undetected typing errors.

You can't do much to reduce the first type of error, although care in selecting programs will help. You can reduce the number of errors of the second type, however. Operating a computer immobilizes many muscles of the body while using others in a manner guaranteed to cause strain and fatigue. And with strain and fatigue come errors.

The strain, the fatigue, and the errors are avoidable, but that means paying as much attention to your desk as to your disks, as much attention to lighting as to the printer, and as much to stretching your muscles as to cleaning the computer room. In short, you should pay as much attention to ergonomics as to hardware and software.

Ergonomics comes from the Greek word for "work." In the present context, it means being concerned with the computer operator as well as the operation of the computer. While some ergonomic measures can be expensive, most involve minimal cost. Ignoring ergonomics, however, can be costly in terms of lost data, lost money, and poor health.

The problem is a lack of adjustment to the computer. Imagine the effect on our bodies if today's automobiles were the ergonomic equivalent of the horse-drawn carriages of the last century. Solid tires, nonadjustable seats, and the lack of windshields would have us screaming for mercy.

Communications guru Marshall McLuhan wrote, "We impose the form of the old on the content of the new. When faced with a totally new situation, we tend always to attach ourselves to the objects, to the flavor of the most recent past. We look at the present through a rearview mirror." The first cars are one example of this phenomenon; only gradually did we adapt them to human operators.

Today the computer is where the automobile was 75 years ago, but with a significant difference. Just after the introduction of automobiles, only a few people used them, and most drivers did not use cars for hours on end, day in and day out. The transition was gradual. But the transition to computers has been rapid and our use of them more prolonged and intense—our eyes and backs are often left aching.

One concern about working with a computer is the possibility that a monitor may emit harmful radiation. The vast majority of computer monitors contain *cathode ray tubes* (CRTs), which are similar to television picture tubes. (Only computers that have "flat" screens, such as an LED or a plasma display, do not have CRTs.) All CRTs emit some radiation, and limited studies have been conducted to determine whether these emissions are harmful. Although one 1983 study by the National Academy of Sciences failed to confirm any specific health problems resulting from using a computer monitor, the subject remains controversial and test results remain inconclusive. A detailed discussion of this topic is presented in "The Radiation Question" (*PC World* magazine, January 1984).

Lighting

A computer is not a typewriter, a screen not a piece of paper. Old-fashioned lighting and furniture are no more appropriate in the modern office than wooden benches and solid tires are on the road. Eyestrain is definitely a problem with staring at a monitor. One factor contributing to eyestrain is focusing at an uncomfortable distance. You can't do anything about this distance with many computers, because the screen and keyboard are attached. But the PC allows you to move the screen independently of the keyboard, to adjust the eye-to-screen distance until it is comfortable.

If you wear glasses or contact lenses, especially if you are over 40, be sure that they are ground for the proper distance. Since we usually focus either very closely for reading or at much greater distance, prescriptions are usually optimized for extremes of vision, often leaving a gap in the middle, right where the screen is located. Bifocals usually require wearers to tilt their heads at an uncomfortable angle. If you wear them, you might want to get a pair of single-vision glasses for computer use.

Another factor contributing to eyestrain is fixed focus—looking at a certain fixed distance over a long period of time. Typewriters force you to refocus every time you reach the end of a page, but using a computer, you can stare at the screen for longer periods without realizing it. Like moths attracted to light, we are drawn to the screen. Give your eyes a rest. Look up every few minutes—across the room or out the window—or close your eyes.

Another cause of eyestrain is excessive glare. You can reduce the ambient light level, adjust the position of the screen and the room lights, or add a glare shield. Since the optimum lighting for viewing a computer screen is considerably less than for most other office work, the first step is lowering the room lighting. Doing so will reduce reflections and allow you to reduce the screen's brightness. Lowering brightness will reduce contrast, making the images easier to look at and the characters sharper.

You may find that moving lamps or the screen just a few inches reduces glare considerably. But unless you have the luxury of dedicating a room solely to computer use, some glare is inevitable. This is where a glare shield comes in. The monochrome monitor actually has some built-in glare protection. The inside surface of the screen is etched, thereby diffusing any light that strikes it. But you may want more protection. Several types of external glare shields are available for the PC. Placing one of these over your screen reduces glare, making long work sessions less fatiguing.

One common type of shield is a fine nylon mesh held taut by a frame. These shields are relatively inexpensive and provide significant glare reduction. The only drawback is that they create a slightly fuzzy image. Several companies also manufacture plastic and glass filters for the monitor. The best ones are constructed of laminated glass with a plastic frame; they attach easily to any monitor and eliminate up to 94 percent of all glare. Glare shield prices range from $20 to $100.

Using a visor for the screen is another way to reduce glare. You can buy a commercially made unit or make one from a few pieces of cardboard. See where the light is coming from, and construct a visor that blocks that light from hitting the screen. Paint it with flat black paint. Don't make the visor too deep, or you'll feel like you're staring into a tunnel.

Another cause of eyestrain is excessive contrast. If you are using the IBM monochrome monitor or another one that has a contrast control (the upper knob on the PC), adjust it until the screen is comfortable for your eyes. The main villain, however, is daylight. The light streaming in through an uncovered window can be more than 100 times as bright as that coming from the screen. If your computer is in front of the window, asking your eyes to adjust to such extremes falls under the category of cruel and unusual punishment. Close the drapes, or turn your desk 90 degrees, and you'll be amazed at the improvement in eye comfort. And never position the computer so the window is directly behind you, or you'll be looking at the window's reflection.

Another factor of eyestrain is the quality of the image generated by the monitor. If you need color for your system, an RGB monitor is preferable to a TV or a composite monitor. But color monitors lack the sharpness of first-rate monochrome monitors. If you regularly spend long hours in front of the computer, consider switching to monochrome or using two screens: color for graphics and monochrome for text. For the best possible image, use the IBM monochrome monitor with a glare shield, adjust the brightness and contrast controls to suit the lighting in your room, and readjust them when the lighting changes.

Although the much-ballyhooed European standards for video terminals specify an amber screen, amber is preferable only in brightly lit environments. With lower ambient light levels you are likely to be more comfortable with a green screen.

Furniture

Back, neck, and shoulder pain or stiffness are common complaints among people who use computers for extended periods. As with glare, these problems can usually be attributed to the computer's setup. A little effort in creating a comfortable work environment will go a long way toward making your use of the computer more productive and enjoyable. Recent studies indicate that the use of ergonomically designed computer furniture in business increases productivity and reduces absenteeism and turnover.

Desks   Does your PC sit on top of the same desk you previously used for paperwork? Is the system unit in front of you, with the monitor on top of it and the keyboard directly in front of you? Unless you are very tall or your desktop is very low, that puts the screen at an angle guaranteed to be a pain in the neck. It also puts the keyboard at a level and an angle that will generate both fatigue and errors. Since the PC lets you position the various components for maximum comfort and efficiency, take advantage of that built-in flexibility.

The top of the screen should be at eye level or slightly lower, so that you look down at about a 15-degree angle to view the screen. The keyboard should be lower than the usual desk height: 26 to 27 inches. Either lower the entire desk or have a separate section for the keyboard. The best arrangement is to have the keyboard on a "breadboard," a flat drawer that slides out when the computer is in use and disappears when it isn't. The desktop can still be 29 to 30 inches high and the keyboard 3 to 4 inches lower.

You can put the system unit off to the side or on a shelf to get it off your work space, and place the monitor directly on the desk-top. (The cables that connect the monitor and system unit will limit placement flexibility somewhat.) If this setup puts the monitor too low, you can either make a base for it or buy a pedestal. A pedestal not only allows you set the monitor at a comfortable height, but by allowing you to change the tilt from time to time, it lets you vary the position of your neck. It can also simplify those slight adjustments that often eliminate reflections on the screen. The pedestals designed for the PC differ in design and height; most offer 360 degrees of swivel, and some offer about 15 degrees of tilt.

Chairs   Several years ago I bought a beautiful $300 oak desk chair that had a high, curved back and gracefully carved arms. It provided an abundance of ego gratification, typing errors, and back pain. The chair's arms forced my arms into an awkward position, and the back offered no support for my back. But the chair was so impressive that it took me over a year and several visits to a chiropractor to admit my mistake. I replaced it with a $70 secretarial chair that, while still short of ideal, has been a major improvement.

A computer chair should offer support. An adjustable backrest is helpful; ideally, a backrest should include an ergonomically designed lumbar support. Traditional secretarial chairs rest on a four-legged base, which allows some instability; the newer five-spoke design, while certainly not essential, tends to be more stable.

A chair should also offer flexibility. You should be able to adjust it to both your size and shape. Some chairs can be adjusted while you remain seated. Such adjustments enable you to fine tune the fit and also vary your position during a long work session as you would adjust your car seat during a long drive. The best chairs provide five adjustments: seat height, back height, backrest movement, backrest flexibility, and seat tilt.

Your chair should move easily and remain clear of the desk as you move around. Your arms should hang freely from your shoulders while you are using the keyboard, so avoid chairs with arms. If you must have arms, make sure that they are low enough or spaced widely enough so they do not interfere with your elbows or forearms while you type.

The chair should also have the right amount of cushioning: too little, and you'll be ready for a break before you really get started; too much, and you'll be wallowing around without adequate support. The padding should be firm.

If a regular chair doesn't solve your problems, you might try an innovative chair from Norway that dispenses with the backrest altogether. You sit on a cushioned seat with your shins pressing against a second cushion; your weight is distributed between the two. Proponents claim that the back automatically assumes a stable, stress-free position.

Accessories

As noted previously, the PC keyboard's nonstandard locations for some keys, particularly <Enter> and the left <Shift> key, take some getting used to. If you find that you can't get used to these locations, perhaps because you use both the PC and a standard typewriter, you might consider a replacement keyboard. For between $200 and $300 you can buy a keyboard that plugs into the PC and provides all the same features but relocates the keys to their traditional positions. These keyboards also include indicator lights on the <CapsLock>, <NumLock>, and other toggle keys (a helpful feature not built into the PC keyboard). They have a different feel than the IBM keyboard, so if you're thinking of buying one, try it out first.

Most typewriters provide larger keys for the carriage return and some of the other functions so your fingers can find them easily. Except for the space bar, all the keytops on the PC are the same size. For about $20 you can buy a set of press-on caps or collars that increase the size of the <Enter>, <Shift>, <Tab>, and <Backspace> keys.

Another inexpensive keyboard enhancement is a plastic template that fits over the keyboard like a wide frame and has information about the function and control keys. They are available for DOS, BASIC, and many popular applications programs. This kind of quick-reference information can save you from having to dig out the manual every time you forget a command.

Another way to improve your keyboard is by using a utility program that enables you to redefine the keys. Some of these programs let you assign strings of characters or commands to individual function keys or <Ctrl> or <Alt> key combinations. Others let you reassign individual keys, in effect changing their locations. If you don't like IBM's nonstandard placement of the left <Shift> key, for example, you can swap it with the <Backslash> key, thereby returning <Shift> to its normal position. You can even redefine the entire keyboard, perhaps changing it from the standard "qwerty" arrangement into the more efficient Dvorak keyboard. Some keyboard utilities offer additional features, such as displaying an on-screen message when <CapsLock> or <NumLock> is engaged.

You will probably have a variety of written materials scattered around your desk when you use the PC. Keeping papers flat on the desk makes them difficult to read, and having to look down every time you shift your gaze from screen to paper strains the neck muscles as well as reducing efficiency. Office supply stores carry various copy holders that can eliminate these difficulties. One type is a small easel that sits on the desk, supporting your work at a comfortable angle. Another is a swinging-arm holder that clamps onto the side or the back of the desk.

Exercise

Even if you have the perfect, ergonomically designed work station, if you sit in the same position long enough, you'll end up with sore muscles. Regular exercise and periodic breaks will go a long way toward preventing sore backs, necks, and shoulders. Any stretching or exercise will help. Following are a few easy exercises that will help loosen and stretch muscle areas that often cause problems. If you regularly have problems with a particular area of your body, ask your physician or chiropractor to recommend specific exercises.

Here are three exercises that you can do without even getting up from the computer. Whenever I have to wait while my PC accesses a disk, I do one of them.

Neck roll   Let your head fall forward so your chin rests on your chest. Then, letting gravity and your head's own weight provide the stretching, slowly roll your head to the left, back, right, and around to its starting point, then reverse the direction.

Back arch   The shoulder and the upper back area should be stretched in both directions. One stretch involves pulling your shoulders back as far as you can, raising your chin as far as possible, and thrusting your chest forward. Concentrate on arching the part of your spine that runs from your mid-back up to the top of your neck.

Shoulder lift While keeping your neck muscles relaxed, lift each shoulder and lower it a few times. Then lift both shoulders together and gently roll them forward and backward in circles to loosen these often tense muscles.

To stretch another common trouble zone, the lumbar region of the lower back, you will have to briefly bid adieu to your PC. Lean against a wall, with your feet about 18 inches from the wall. Raise one knee, and use your hands to pull the knee toward your chest. Hold it for several seconds, slowly lower it, and repeat with the other leg. This exercise is even more effective if you lie on your back and stretch one leg at a time or both together.

In today's computer environment the old gag, "Put your shoulder to the wheel, your ear to the ground, and your nose to the grindstone; now try to work in that position," doesn't seem as funny as it once did. To work effectively with a computer—or with any other tool—you should take care to establish a work place that is both comfortable and efficient. Even though the computer may be doing much of the actual work, your own comfort and efficiency must be the primary concerns in creating and maintaining this environment.

The PC Community

By now you should be reasonably at home with the computer, with PC-DOS, and, at least in a general way, with programs and programming. You can now use the IBM PC or XT and take advantage of the resources available in the PC community: a multitude of books and magazines covering the PC and PC-specific programs; seminars, tapes, and training guides to help you learn procedures and programs; and a network of PC users who exchange information and advice.

Literature

As computers have gained wide acceptance for both business and personal use, the literature about them has proliferated. No matter what your special interests or your level of computer experience, you will find books and magazines that will help you make better use of this sophisticated tool.

Books   When I got my first computer, I bought every book I could find that covered word processing. The total cost was around $70. Today you could spend more than that for books on a single program. For the price of all the IBM PC books, you could probably buy a disk drive or dot matrix printer. Obviously, you can't buy them all, and even if you could, you would never have enough time to read them. But reading the right books and building your own computer library are some of the best investments you can make.

Books for personal computer users fall into five categories: general, machine specific, task specific, program specific, and programming. The general books tend to have titles like "Computers for Everybody," "Guide to Personal Computing," and "The Personal Computer Book." If you own or have used a computer or have read at least two computer books, many of your friends will consider you an expert and seek your advice. Instead of recommending a computer, recommend a book. If they end up with a lemon, they won't blame you. The existence of machine-specific books is one of the advantages of choosing an IBM PC. The first computer I owned was an excellent machine, but it didn't generate a community of helpful books and user networks. Problems that I could have solved by reading a few pages in the right book took me hours or days to unravel.

Take advantage of the wealth of PC-oriented books—buy several. But before opening your wallet, open each book and ask a few questions. How timely is the book? Some books still on the shelves were written for single-sided drives or early versions of PC-DOS. What does the book cover and in how much depth? Some books focus on applications programs, while others cover printers or advanced aspects of the system's design. Some machine-specific books devote 30 to 80 percent of their pages to teaching BASIC programming. If you are not interested in programming, don't buy one of these books. And if you want to learn about programming, you might want to pass up a book that devotes one chapter to it in favor of one devoted entirely to that topic.

How original is the book? In the rush to enter the marketplace, many authors use material from other books they have written or from other sources. So you might end up with a book originally written for the Atari that has had just enough PC-specific information added to it to justify "IBM" on the cover. Or you might find page after page taken straight out of the manuals you already own. Unless you trust the author, the publisher, or the person who recommended the book, browse through it carefully before heading to the cash register.

Some task-specific books are primarily buyer's guides. Examples are David Kruglinski's *Data Base Management Systems* (Osborne/McGraw-Hill) and Hal Glatzer's *Introduction to Word Processing* (Sybex). These books introduce you to a task such as data base management or word processing and help select a program to accomplish that task. While some evaluate particular programs, others analyze features, so you can do your own evaluations. Other task-specific books are more concerned with accomplishing a task than choosing a program. For example, *Writing in the Computer Age* (Doubleday) by Andrew Fluegelman and Jeremy Joan Hewes devotes most of its pages to using a word processor and is useful for people who already have one.

Closely related are program-specific books. These books are tutorials devoted to a single program. They usually cover much the same ground as the program's documentation but often in a more understandable fashion. They often include valuable tips gleaned from using the program over a long period of time.

Of the programming books, the largest number deal with BASIC, but you'll have no trouble finding books on Pascal, COBOL, FORTRAN, and various other languages. Many of these texts are intended for classroom use. Look for one that takes a tutorial approach and guides you step-by-step. Avoid the reference books and the fill-in-the-blanks books that familiarize you with a language but don't actually get you programming. While most programming books are generic, it's best to find one specific to the IBM PC.

Magazines In the past few years the number of computer magazines has grown at a rate equaled only by computer books and McDonald's franchises. Like the books, these magazines run the gamut from general to specific, elementary to advanced, excellent to terrible.

Since there are several magazines that focus on the IBM PC, it certainly makes sense to subscribe to one or two of them. Magazines such as *PC World* and *Softalk* review software and accessories for the PC, pass along operating tips, publish tutorials, and familiarize you with the various uses people are making of their PCs.

You might also want to subscribe to one of the more general magazines. They range from elementary (*Micro Discovery*) to advanced (*BYTE*). Two that are fairly diverse in their coverage are *Popular Computing* and *Personal Computing*. But don't get a two-year subscription to a magazine that you may outgrow in six months. The best way to stay on top of the latest developments in the field is by reading the weekly microcomputer news magazine, *InfoWorld*.

Several magazines are directed toward business rather than home computer use. *Business Computer Systems, Business Software,* and *Interface Age* are three examples. Other publications, such as *WP News* (word processing) and *dNotes* (*dBASE II*) focus on particular applications or programs.

The multitude of new programs, add-on hardware, and accessories make the ads in these magazines particularly useful. Many magazines include reader service cards that simplify obtaining additional information about the products that interest you.

Documentation   The breakthrough that I await most eagerly is not a pocket-sized PC compatible, a hard disk priced at under $500, or a monitor whose resolution equals *National Geographic*'s; it is readable documentation. The other three may arrive first.

The very term documentation is an indication that something is amiss. We need more than point-by-point coverage of the details of a hardware or software system—instructions, a guide, something that helps us use the program. "Documentation" sounds like something for technical experts, and unfortunately, it often is.

Documentation for hardware or software should do several things. It should orient us to the system it accompanies by providing an overview of what that system does, what its components are, and how those parts are related. And because we learn to use equipment and programs by actually using them, documentation should provide step-by-step tutorials. It should also serve as a comprehensive reference that we can consult whenever we have a question or run into problems.

Take IBM's PC-DOS manual, for example. As an overview, it is almost worthless. Like most documentation, this manual was apparently written by people who knew the system so well that they couldn't put themselves in the place of someone who doesn't know it.

The DOS manual provides some tutorial material, but the learning is by rote, without an adequate understanding of what you are doing or why. Looking at the way the manual is organized, you can see that it was never intended as an introductory book. The bulk of the volume is in neither a learning sequence nor a logical order but alphabetical order. It is designed for retrieval, not teaching.

As reference books, the DOS and BASIC manuals are superb. But PC users need other books that provide an overview or tutorials. The PC's *Guide to Operations* is a little better than the DOS manual in the overview and tutorial departments, but it is less comprehensive as a reference source.

Be aware of what a given set of documentation does and doesn't provide. Many PC owners who are disappointed that the IBM manuals don't explain things clearly enough never refer to them again. This is a mistake. As reference books they are relatively clear and complete. But although you can learn DOS and BASIC from them, you can't learn either in an easy or effective manner.

Yet no matter how poor a piece of documentation may be, you are likely to discover things by reading it that you will learn nowhere else. You don't have to go through it in one sitting, but make sure that you read it all eventually.

Training

In addition to studying books, magazines, and documentation, you can accelerate your computer learning by taking classes or using some of the various training aids on the market.

Classes   Whether you take a "class," a "workshop," or a "seminar," having a live instructor in front of you can be the fastest way to learn a new subject. It can also be the most expensive. But if you figure in the value of your time, this form of instruction may actually turn out to be the least expensive.

To locate computer classes, start by checking the local computer stores. If dealers don't offer classes themselves, they may know who does. Also contact the continuing education office of nearby colleges or universities. In addition to semester-long courses, you'll probably find a choice of shorter courses that cover the topic in a session or two.

Before signing up for a course, however, make sure that it will be worth your investment in both time and money. Is the content appropriate? The range of topics is as wide as that of books, so you'll have to browse a bit to make your choice. If the brochures don't give you a clear idea of the content, you can make a few phone calls, track down the instructor, and get your questions answered.

Is the instructor appropriate? Because computer training is in such demand, many courses are staffed with unqualified instructors. Teaching a computer course demands expertise in both the subject matter and in teaching. It doesn't matter how much the instructor knows if he or she can't communicate it. Although far from foolproof, one measure of proficiency is how many times the person has taught the course; let the instructor work out the bugs on someone else.

Are the facilities appropriate? Some topics can be handled well in standard lecture format. Others can be learned best if the students actually apply the information on the spot, working with a computer under an instructor's direction. If the course purports to be "hands on," find out how many hands; one student per computer is ideal, two is workable, but more than two usually is not.

Training aids   While classes are useful, you may not find one that meets your needs or fits your schedule. An alternative is lessons packaged in disk or cassette form. A wide range of tutorials are available on floppy disks, audio cassettes, and videocassettes, and a few are available on videodiscs. In addition to being more accessible than live classes, these learning aids have the advantage of allowing you to go through the material at your own pace and review as often as you want.

Tutorials are available for the fundamentals of the PC, DOS, and many programs. As with books and classes, the quality varies, so look before you leap. Avoid products that merely imitate books. Look for tutorials that are "interactive": they present information, ask you to apply that information, and then respond to what you did. Some disk-based tutorials devote part of the screen to instruction and the remainder to a simulation of the program being taught. You get hands-on experience with the program while avoiding the usual trial-and-error fumbling.

Although audio cassettes lack interaction, they can provide excellent step-by-step instruction. They also offer the freedom of reviewing a lesson while you do other things such as driving your car or doing the dishes, and they are relatively inexpensive. A few even present fundamental information on one side and more specialized instruction or even a test on the other side of the cassette.

Videocassettes (and videodiscs) provide both audio and visual instruction. Some are designed to interface with the computer, with the video presentation keyed to your activity on the keyboard. The equipment required is expensive, but if you already own a video player, this option is worth considering.

PC Networks

The ultimate PC resource is networks: people with whom you can share information. There are informal networks for a variety of professions, special interests, and geographical areas. Even if you can't find one right away, you can start one on a small scale and watch it grow. If you meet someone who has similar equipment, programs, or interests at a computer store, a computer fair, or in the adjoining seat on a bus or an airplane, trade phone numbers. When you come across information your colleague might need, pass it on. You're likely to find that he or she will do the same. If you take computer classes, pass around a networking sheet, photocopy it, and distribute it. Make a note of which people in the class ask questions related to your own concerns, then seek them out.

There are also formal organizations, PC user groups. User groups are more prevalent in metropolitan areas, but their numbers are growing throughout the country. By August 1983, two years after IBM introduced the PC, more than 100 user groups were scattered among 40 states and 6 Canadian provinces.

In addition to a speaker, a demonstration, or another organized program, user group meetings usually have "random access" sessions in which members ask questions and exchange tips and information. Meetings usually break up into special interest groups (SIGs). These small groups often post signs identifying their subject matter, so you can easily wander from group to group. There are

SIGs for specific programs (such as *1-2-3, dBASE II,* or *WordStar*), types of programs (such as investment software or games), programming languages, education, and communications. All it takes to form a SIG is one member suggesting it and one or more others responding to the suggestion.

Many PC user groups publish newsletters ranging from one-page meeting announcements to full-blown magazines complete with product reviews, articles, and columns. Most groups maintain a library of public-domain programs, which the club librarian duplicates and sells at meetings for a little more than the cost of the disk. Not many applications programs turn up in these collections, but they usually include utilities and games.

Some user groups, and a number of dedicated individuals, sponsor electronic bulletin boards. These on-line message centers often provide public-domain software, which any caller can copy to his or her own system via modem and phone line. Bulletin board services (BBSs) are free except for the cost of the phone call, and they are a true source of networking. If you don't know of a PC user group in your area, ask local computer stores, or check *User Group Dispatch* and *BBS Watch* in *PC World* magazine for lists of user groups and bulletin boards.

Play

Even if you bought a PC strictly for work, you can still have fun with it. You don't have to plow through the documentation every time you're not sure how to do something. If you have an idea, try it out. You can't hurt the computer from the keyboard, so, assuming you have backed up your work, experiment. The more you enjoy the computer, the better you'll get to know it, and the more effective a tool it will become.

A colleague called me last week after trying unsuccessfully to use her PC and a modem to communicate with a nearby university's mainframe computer. "It's been one of those days when I didn't get a thing done, but I learned a lot," she told me. Days like that are sometimes more valuable than the painless ones.

A Glimpse into the Silicon Ball

Pac-Man is not America's favorite computer game—Speculate is. The rules are simple. The first player speculates about an advanced feature that will be available soon or an alleged reduced price for a currently available feature. Then the other players try to top the first player. Speculate can be played at home, at work, or in the media. The prize is dissatisfaction. A few rounds of Speculate will convince you that the computer that just accomplished in 45 minutes what used to take you three days is woefully inadequate.

In a sense, all computers are either experimental or obsolete. Or as one Speculate champion put it, "If it works, it's obsolete." But before you give up and trade your PC for an abacus, there is another way to view computer developments. The fact that a new computer may be smaller on the outside, bigger on the inside, faster, less expensive, or promoted by a more popular TV star doesn't change your computer's capabilities. A computer that does the job you need done is not obsolete. Obviously, computers will increase in speed and capacity and be reduced in price and size. But when? How? How much?

Your IBM PC or XT, however configured, should give you years of service. And should you want to add new features, the PC's modular construction makes it easy. In all likelihood, by the time you need to replace the PC, it will have paid for itself many times over. Be a spectator, not a player, in Speculate. Rather than worrying about what's coming next, learn to tap the vast power of the computer you already have.

Appendix: Products and Manufacturers

Following is a list of programs mentioned in this book. The memory requirements listed are for DOS 2.00.

1-2-3
Lotus Development Corporation
161 First St.
Cambridge, MA 02142
617/492-7171
Requirements: 192K, two disk drives;
color graphics board or dot matrix printer
to use graphics component

AbStat
Anderson-Bell
P.O. Box 191
Canon City, CO 81212
303/275-1661
Requirements: 128K, two disk drives

dBASE II
Ashton-Tate
10150 W. Jefferson Blvd.
Culver City, CA 90230
213/204-5570
Requirements: 128K, one disk drive

DesQ
Quarterdeck Office Systems
1918 Main St.
Santa Monica, CA 90405
800/845-6621, 213/392-9852
Requirements: 320K (512K recommended),
5M hard disk; mouse optional

Diskette Librarian
IBM
Systems Products Division
P.O. Box 1328
Boca Raton, FL 33432
800/447-4700; 800/447-0890
Alaska, Hawaii
Requirements: 64K, one disk drive

Diskette Manager
Lassen Software, Inc.
P.O. Box 1190
Chico, CA 95927
916/891-6957
Requirements: 128K, 80-character monitor, two disk drives to access all functions (label printing and catalog), one drive to print labels only

EasyFiler
Information Unlimited Software
2401 Marinship Way
Sausalito, CA 94965
415/331-6700
Requirements: 96K, two disk drives

EasyWriter II
Information Unlimited Software
2401 Marinship Way
Sausalito, CA 94965
415/331-6700
Requirements: 128K, two disk drives
Note: *EasyWriter II* is now part of the *EasyWriter II System,* an integrated word processing, spelling checker, and mail-merge program. *EasyWriter II* is no longer sold separately.

Executive Suite
Armonk Corporation
204 7th St.
Balboa, CA 92661
714/673-7520
Requirements: 64K, one disk drive

InfoStar
MicroPro International Corporation
33 San Pablo Ave.
San Rafael, CA 94903
415/499-1200
Requirements: 96K, two disk drives (hard disk recommended)

MBA
Context Management Systems
23868 Hawthorne Blvd.
Torrance, CA 90505
213/378-8277
Requirements: 256K, two disk drives, IBM Color/Graphics Adapter

Spellbinder
Lexisoft, Inc.
P.O. Box 1378
Davis, CA 95617
916/758-3630
Requirements: 128K, two disk drives

Super Chartman II
Mosaic Software, Inc.
1972 Massachusetts Ave.
Cambridge, MA 02140
617/491-2434
Requirements: 128K, two disk drives,
color/graphics board (not high resolution)

Survtab
Statistical Computing Consultants
10037 Chestnut Wood Ln.
Burke, VA 22015
703/250-9513
Requirements: 64K, one disk drive

ThinkTank
Living Videotext, Inc.
1000 Elwell Ct.
Palo Alto, CA 94303
415/964-6300
Requirements: 256K, two disk drives or
one floppy disk drive and a hard disk

Microsoft Windows
Microsoft Corporation
10700 Northup Way
Bellevue, WA 98004
206/828-8080
Requirements: 192K, two disk drives,
pointing device

Millionaire
Blue Chip Software, Inc.
6744 Eton Ave.
Canoga Park, CA 91304
818/346-0730
Requirements: 64K, one disk drive

PC-Talk III
The Headlands Press, Inc.
P.O. Box 862
Tiburon, CA 94920
415/435-9775
Requirements: 64K (128K for compiled
version), one disk drive

**The PromptDoc Document Management
System (formerly First Draft)**
PromptDoc, Inc.
833 W. Colorado Ave. #113
Colorado Springs, CO 80905
303/471-9875
Requirements: 64K, two disk drives or
one floppy disk drive and a hard disk,
80-column monitor

Typing Tutor
IBM
Systems Products Division
P.O. Box 1328
Boca Raton, FL 33432
800/447-4700; 800/447-0890 Alaska,
Hawaii
Requirements: 48K, one disk drive
Note: An enhanced version of this pro-
gram, *Typing Tutor III,* is available from
Simon & Schuster.

VisiCalc
VisiCorp
2895 Zanker Rd.
San Jose, CA 95134
408/946-9000
Requirements: 64K, one disk drive

Visi On
VisiCorp
2895 Zanker Rd.
San Jose, CA 95134
408/946-9000
Requirements: one floppy disk drive, one
hard disk; graphics board and graphics
monitor to run windows

WordStar
MicroPro International Corporation
33 San Pablo Ave.
San Rafael, CA 94903
415/499-1200
Requirements: 64K, one disk drive

The IBM PC and XT are available from:
IBM
Systems Products Division
P.O. Box 1328
Boca Raton, FL 33432
800/447-4700; 800/447-0890 Alaska,
Hawaii

David Arnold is Professor of Sociology and former Chair of the Sociology Department at Sonoma State University, where he teaches a course on Computers and Society. He has published numerous articles on computers, sociology, photography, aviation, travel, and other topics. He is author of *The Sociology of Subcultures,* and has also written a book about the IBM PCjr.

The following people contributed to this book:

Editor: Jeremy Joan Hewes; *Consulting Editors, PC World*: David Bunnell, Andrew Fluegelman, Eric Brown; *Consulting Editor, Simon & Schuster*: Robert C. Eckhardt; *PC World Books Editorial staff*: Betsy Dilernia, Evelyn Spire, Lindy Wankoff, Seth Novogrodsky, Joanne Clapp; *Production Director*: Jacqueline Poitier; *Designer*: Marjorie Spiegelman; *Art Director*: Bruce Charonnat; *Production and Art staff*: Ellyn Hament, Jim Felici, Rebecca Oliver, Dennis McLeod, Monica Thorsnes, Darcy Blake, Donna Sharee; *Photographer*: David Bishop; *Cover Photographer*: Fred Stimson; *Typesetter*: Design & Type, San Francisco.

Each of the following products in italics is a trademark or a registered trademark of the company listed in parentheses after the product name: *1-2-3* (Lotus Development Corporation), *AbStat* (Anderson-Bell), *dBASE II* (Ashton-Tate), *DesQ* (Quarterdeck Office Systems), *Diskette Librarian* (IBM), *Diskette Manager* (Lassen Software, Inc.), *EasyFiler* (Information Unlimited Software), *EasyWriter II* (Information Unlimited Software), *Executive Suite* (Armonk Corporation), *IBM Personal Computer* and *XT* (International Business Machines Corp.), *InfoStar* (MicroPro International Corporation), *MBA* (Context Management Systems), *Microsoft Windows* (Microsoft Corporation), *Millionaire* (Blue Chip Software, Inc.), *PC-Talk III* (The Headlands Press, Inc.), *The PromptDoc Document Management System* (PromptDoc, Inc.), *Spellbinder* (Lexisoft, Inc.), *Super Chartman II* (Mosaic Software, Inc.), *Survtab* (Statistical Computing Consultants), *ThinkTank* (Living Videotext, Inc.), *Typing Tutor* (IBM), *VisiCalc* (VisiCorp), *Visi On* (VisiCorp), *WordStar* (MicroPro International Corporation).

IBM is a registered trademark of International Business Machines Corp.

The instructions and exercises in this book have been developed and tested by the authors and publisher. The authors and publisher make no expressed or implied warranty regarding the contents of the book.

Index

Page numbers in *italic* indicate
definitions.

Other Books in the PC World Library

How to Buy an IBM PC, XT, or PC-Compatible Computer

by Danny Goodman and the Editors of PC World

More people buy the IBM PC and PC-compatibles than any other personal computers. But the PC and compatibles come in many configurations for many different tasks, and selecting an appropriate system is not always easy. This book is the only guide you will need, and it will save you hours of unnecessary effort and confusion. *How to Buy an IBM PC, XT, or PC-Compatible Computer* answers all the questions that frustrate buyers. It also addresses many other important ones that are often overlooked, such as how to match the system to the work it must perform (including decisions about memory size, type of disk drives, displays and printers, conservation of expansion slots, and choice of essential software), evaluating dealers and salespeople, and selecting a maintenance organization and contract. In addition, the authors provide an extensive discussion of the complex issue of PC compatibility and offer reviews of the most important PC-compatible computers. In today's crowded and confusing computer marketplace, *How to Buy an IBM PC, XT, or PC-Compatible Computer* is an excellent guide to making sensible purchasing decisions.
Available May 1984

Hardware for the IBM PC and XT

by Frederic E. Davis and the Editors of PC World

Hardware for the IBM PC and XT is an invaluable guide and reference that will help you make sense of the continually expanding and sometimes perplexing array of add-on equipment available for the PC, XT, and PC-compatible computers. If you're a newcomer to the PC, the general introductions to peripherals—from such familiar items as keyboards, game controllers, and monitors to more exotic devices such as voice recognition devices, bubble memory, and graphics plotters—will provide a solid starting point for understanding each type of hardware. If you already know how you want to expand your system, you can consult the comprehensive listings of the major brand-name products to narrow down your choices. Each product listing contains a complete description of the peripheral and its capabilities, as well as a discussion of the important criteria for evaluating its features. There are also sections on troubleshooting any problems that might occur with peripherals and on designing efficient computer work areas. In short, *Hardware for the IBM PC and XT* opens up new worlds of personal computing by helping you expand your system sensibly, efficiently, and precisely to your needs.
Available June 1984

Getting Started with the IBM PCjr

by David Myers and the Editors of PC World

In the same way that the IBM PC has become the dominant force in personal computers, the IBM Home Computer—the PCjr—is emerging as an equally exciting and impressive force among family-oriented machines. To introduce you to the PCjr, and to computing in general, David Myers and the Editors of PC World have applied their expertise to describing this fascinating machine, providing you and your family with the perfect guide to making the most of your PCjr. *Getting Started with the IBM PCjr* includes detailed and easy-to-understand instructions for using the cordless keyboard, color monitors, and television sets for exciting graphics displays, the disk operating system, cartridge and disk-based software, and all of the most important peripherals that expand the PCjr's capabilities, such as printers, light pens, modems, joysticks, and much more. Special features of the PCjr are highlighted by hands-on tutorials covering graphics and music, and the use of BASIC and Logo. The book also explains how to access information services such as The Source and CompuServe through your telephone. *Getting Started with the IBM PCjr* will help enable you to make home computing one of life's simple pleasures.
Available August 1984

**Desktop Applications
for the IBM PC and XT**

*by Patrick Plemmons and
the Editors of PC World*

Most people buy a personal computer for just one activity, such as word processing, financial calculations, or information management. In doing so, they fail to use the computer's innate capacity to perform many other types of tasks equally efficiently and effectively. The purpose of *Desktop Applications for the IBM PC and XT* is to demonstrate the amazing breadth and power of a PC, and to help you take advantage of the computer's potential as both a personal and a professional tool. The book explains in clear and comprehensive terms the principal categories of professional computer applications: spreadsheets, word processing, data base management, accounting and financial programs, graphics, and integrated software, which performs several functions and can transfer information quickly and easily between applications. In addition, the authors show you how to make the best use of the computer to execute these tasks. You will learn about the major software packages in each applications category, and how to match tasks to the appropriate software. *Desktop Applications for the IBM PC and XT* is certain to expand your knowledge of computing and the uses for your PC or XT.
Available September 1984

**Communications for the
IBM PC and XT**

*by Lisa Stahr and the
Editors of PC World*

One of the truly exciting features of personal computers is their ability to exchange information with each other—and with distant mainframe computers—over the telephone lines. *Communications for the IBM PC and XT* provides a window on resources that extend beyond your PC alone. Clear, comprehensive, and thought-provoking, the book explains how to select the most appropriate modem and communications software for your PC and gives you a nontechnical look at how computers actually communicate with one another. The authors also explain how to use the different types of communications to best suit your professional and personal needs, including conducting research on commercial data bases; acquiring software—sometimes for free—by downloading it over the phone lines; sending and receiving messages on an electronic bulletin board; and linking several PCs and XTs into a local area network so that you and your group can access each other's information and thereby perform your work more efficiently than ever. No matter what your specific needs may be, *Communications for the IBM PC and XT* will help you make the most of your computer's ability to join forces with other computers.
Available October 1984

Learning and Having Fun with the IBM PC and PCjr

by Fred D'Ignazio and the Editors of PC World

You may think the IBM PC is all work and no play—not true! *Learning and Having Fun with the IBM PC and PCjr* is a delightful, informative look at the vast array of educational and recreational software available for the IBM PC and PCjr (which was designed for games and learning programs). Fred D'Ignazio and the Editors of PC World look at the main areas of educational and recreational computing—from math and spelling programs to mind-boggling adventures and sophisticated tutorials. They provide criteria for determining what constitutes a good game or learning program and evaluate the best and most important software available today. In addition, the book contains hands-on examples of games and educational programs that will enable you to take advantage of the many features of the PC and PCjr and design your own games. So take a break from your spreadsheets and data bases—don your aviator glasses, or strap on Excalibur—and start *Learning and Having Fun with the IBM PC and PCjr.*
Available November 1984

The Fully Powered PC

by Burton Alperson, Andrew Fluegelman, Lawrence J. Magid, and the Editors of PC World

Now that you own a PC and have been working with it for some time, are you starting to wish it had just a few more special features to help you do your job even better? Perhaps a way to execute a command in one keystroke that now takes six? Or a way to make a section of internal memory act like a disk—but fifty times as fast? Are you running out of expansion slots, even as you can think of a dozen more boards you'd like to add? Relax—and read The *Fully Powered PC*, the first and only guide devoted exclusively to ways of customizing the highly versatile PC with modestly priced software and hardware additions, including keyboard reconfiguration programs, spoolers, custom-designed menus, batch filers, and multi-function expansion boards (to squeeze even more capabilities into one expansion slot). With up-to-the-minute guidance from the experts, you'll be able to create a computer system exactly as you want it. When you're ready to take full advantage of your computing capabilities, shift into high gear with *The Fully Powered PC.*
Available January 1985

LOGO for the PC and PCjr

by David Myers and the Editors of PC World

As the personal computer revolution spreads, more and more computer owners have become aware of Logo, which is rapidly emerging as the language of choice for teaching children the fundamentals of computers, programming, and logical thinking. But did you know that Logo is not just for children, and that it's not just a language that makes it easy to create graphics on your computer? *Logo for the PC and PCjr* leads adults and children alike into the world of Logo programming. The book shows you how this elegant, easy-to-learn language can be used to both understand computers and create practical programs that are not available commercially. Using a hands-on, tutorial approach, David Myers and the Editors of PC World take you beyond most other books on Logo, explaining clearly and completely the many fascinating features of this language, including creating turtle graphics, animating sprites, learning how to define your own Logo commands, and even programming your PC or PCjr to converse with you in plain English. And, of course, *Logo for the PC and PCjr* is filled with many sample Logo programs that are both practical and fun.
Available February 1985

Hands On: Useful Tips and Routines for the IBM PC and XT

by the Editors of PC World

For everyone who enjoys the vast number of practical tips and useful articles that have appeared in *PC World* since its very first issue, the Editors of PC World have collected the best pieces from the "Hands On" and "Star-Dot-Star" sections of the magazine. This book covers both hardware and software, and it is clearly organized so that you can quickly find information on virtually anything you need to know about your PC: instructions for installing boards and disk drives, troubleshooting hardware problems, patching programs to utilize the special features of various printers, and increasing programming efficiency. Additional chapters of the book detail specific program applications, such as creating a checkbook ledger with Lotus *1-2-3*, printing envelopes, labels, and other odd-sized documents with WordStar, keeping tax records on *dBASE II*, and tracking investments with *SuperCalc*. *Hands On* is the definitive collection of "how-to's" for your PC from the true experts in the field, the Editors of PC World.
Available March 1985

☐ **Getting Started with the IBM PC and XT**
by David Arnold and the Editors of PC World
49277-2 $14.95   Available May 1984

☐ **How to Buy an IBM PC, XT, or PC-Compatible Computer**
by Danny Goodman and the Editors of PC World
49282-9 $14.95   Available May 1984

☐ **Hardware for the IBM PC and XT**
by Frederic E. Davis and the Editors of PC World
49277-2 $14.95   Available July 1984

☐ **Getting Started with the IBM PCjr**
by David Myers and the Editors of PC World
49253-5 $12.95   Available August 1984

Prices subject to change without notice.

Simon & Schuster, Inc.
Simon & Schuster Building, 1230 Avenue of the Americas
New York, N.Y. 10020, Mail Order Dept. CP4

Please send me copies of the books checked above.

☐ Please charge to my credit card. _____MasterCard _____Visa

My credit card number is_____ and expires_____

Signature_____

☐ Save! I enclose a check for the full amount; publisher pays postage and handling.

Name (please print)_____

Address_____

City_____ State_____ Zip Code_____

Also available at your local bookstore.